Young Women's Monologs from Contemporary Plays

PROFESSIONAL AUDITIONS FOR ASPIRING ACTRESSES

Edited by
GERALD LEE RATLIFF

mp

MERIWETHER PUBLISHING
A division of Pioneer Drama Service, Inc.
Denver, Colorado

Meriwether Publishing
A division of Pioneer Drama Service, Inc.
PO Box 4267
Englewood, CO 80155

www.pioneerdrama.com

Executive editor: Theodore O. Zapel
Cover design: Jan Melvin

© Copyright 2004 Meriwether Publishing
Printed in the United States of America
First Edition / Hardcover ISBN: 978-1-56608-257-0

The Library of Congress has cataloged the paperback edition as follows:

Young women's monologs from contemporary plays : professional auditions for aspiring actresses / edited with an acting introduction by Gerald Lee Ratliff. -- 1st ed.
    p. cm.
   ISBN 978-1-56608-097-2 (pbk.)
1. Monologues. 2. Acting--Auditions. I. Ratliff, Gerald Lee.
  PN2080.Y69 2004
  812'.045089287 -- dc22
                        2004015757

1   2   3   20   21   22

Contents

Chapter VII
New Age Voices 195

Preface

This collection of monologs for women is suitable for classroom discussion and performance for mid-teens, teens, young adults, and adults. This does not mean, of course, that the monolog characters need to fall into that age range. You may wish to explore performance opportunities that fall outside that age range. There are a number of principles at work in this collection of monologs. Featured authors include well-established writers who voice traditional views on current women's issues and a host of relatively new, contemporary writers who offer fresh and provocative insights on similar topics. The monologs selected for inclusion represent challenging material you might expect to discuss and perform in acting or literature classes, auditions, festivals, contests, or workshops. Each monolog also includes a brief character analysis and an appropriate age range to help promote authentic character portraits in performance.

For ease of reference, chapters are divided into "thematic" ages rather than standard categories that identify characters simply by chronological age, gender, ethnicity, type, or similar points of view. Chapter I, "Classroom Performance and Audition Etiquette," outlines the basic principles at work in choosing a monolog for performance and offers a number of valuable practices to be aware of when preparing for classroom performance or an audition.

Chapter II, "The Age of Innocence," introduces youthful adolescents engaged in childish role-playing games and some mature and strong-willed adults who still cling to their youthful innocence and childhood memories. Chapter III, "Coming of Age," features monolog characters whose experiences have taught them that human nature can be cruel and callous. Chapter IV, "The Age of Rebellion," highlights monolog characters who are often engaged in the struggle for independence and personal values or the conflict between duty to oneself and duty to others.

Chapter V, "The Gilded Age," offers eccentric, flamboyant, and neurotic characters drawn from the everyday world with a comic flair that masks their outrageous behavior. Chapter VI, "The Golden Age," includes more mature, resolute stage figures whose life experiences and values, principles, or morals set them apart from other monolog characters in the collection. You might want to thumb through the table of contents to get a sense of the roles available and then go directly to the brief introduction of each monolog of interest for more critical comments or performance suggestions. Remember as well that you may need to edit some of the longer monolog selections to meet classroom or other performance time limits.

One of the special features of this monolog collection is Chapter VII, "New Age Voices," which introduces monolog characters written specifically for auditions, contests, or public readings. Although these characters are independent and not excerpts from longer scripts, they share many of the life experiences, personal opinions, and points of view expressed by monolog characters in other chapters. In addition, there are a number of duologs, or brief scenes for two performers, included at the end of each chapter to help you polish your performance skills with a partner. Each duolog should encourage you and a partner to work collaboratively in sketching contrasting character portraits that spark of imagination and intuition.

Now a final word about using this collection of monologs. Contemporary plays often deal with serious, sometimes controversial, issues that are voiced in strong language or provocative situations. In this collection of monologs, that language and those situations have been kept to a minimum. With the experience and practical knowledge gained in classroom discussion, you should be able to design a consistent performance "blueprint" most appropriate for your own individual skills and personal views on the issues being addressed by the monolog characters.

Begin the exploration with a blueprint that suits your own age, highlights your vocal range and physical type, promotes movement potential, and encourages your imaginative self-expression in performance. Strive to increase the range and depth of your self-expression by playing multiple monologs with varying ages, vocal ranges, and physical types. You should also approach each monolog or duolog with sensitivity, using a conversational tone of delivery and a relaxed, natural sense of movement.

Gerald Lee Ratliff
May 2004

Chapter I

Classroom Performance and Audition Etiquette

Imagination, Industry, and Intelligence —
the Three I's — are all indispensable to the actor,
but of these three the greatest is,
without any doubt, Imagination.

— Ellen Terry, Memoirs

Before choosing a monolog for the classroom or a formal audition, it is important to understand that there is a performance "etiquette" that should be practiced to help sharpen your competitive edge. For example, the first twenty-five seconds of a monolog may be the most critical in terms of demonstrating your potential range of emotional, physical, and vocal qualities. The last twenty-five seconds of a monolog may be just as crucial to show character development through subtle shifts in gesture, posture, or movement. Although you will probably learn more about performance etiquette through actual classroom and audition experiences, the principles outlined in this introductory chapter should guide you in living within the "stage world" of your monolog character rather than simply acting in an empty classroom or on a bare audition floor.

Understanding and Preparing a Character

Classroom performances or auditions usually rely on brief monologs or excerpts from a longer script to capture a moment-in-time of an individual character's theatrical life. Because you are performing an isolated moment in the character's theatrical life, without the complete script to give the monolog its real context, you must be thoroughly familiar with the character and the character's story in the longer script to accurately depict just one selected episode or event. It is also important to remember that a number of your talents (voice, body, intelligence, imagination, sensitivity, interpretation, and movement) will be on display — simultaneously. It is essential, therefore, that a classroom performance or an audition accurately reflect your natural skills and enhance the monolog character portrait that you are sketching.

Step One

One of the first steps in understanding your character and the story being told is to closely examine the complete script. It is only then that you can intelligently describe what you want the audience to "see" and "hear" in the performance. In telling the character's story, you should be able to answer the following "5 W" questions:

> Who is the character addressing?
>
> What is the character's desire or objective?
>
> Where is the locale or setting?
>
> When does the action climax?
>
> Why is the character speaking now?

The more knowledge you have about the character's story and the complete script, the more possibilities you have for an imaginative classroom performance or audition. At first, it is best to read the complete script with a sense of appreciation to understand the character's attitude or point of view. Then read the script as you might read a short story. Sort out character relationships, chart the flow of events, identify the conflict, and allow the character's story to tell itself in the action, dialog, and stage directions. If possible, try to read the complete script in one sitting and sense the rising momentum of conflict and confrontation as they build to a climax. Pay particular attention to the locale, or setting, and the scenic design that may help you visualize the story being told.

A second reading of the script should be more critical than the first. Focus on background information that may guide your interpretation of the monolog. Reread the primary scenes of the character's interaction with others and identify typical reactions or responses in given situations. Then isolate specific character actions, lines of dialog, mannerisms, and other supporting examples of character attitude, mood, or point of view that may help you refine your interpretation of the monolog. The more analytical second reading of the complete script should suggest possible adjustments that may need to be made in both interpretation and performance.

Continued reading of the script should help you polish the interpretation and the performance, especially in terms of easily identifying the behavioral pattern of reactions and responses. Frequent rereading of the script should also encourage a character voice and body to emerge, reveal movements, gestures, and physical actions that may help to visualize the character, and suggest a stage presence that will give life and vitality to your character in performance.

Step Two

The second step in preparing a classroom performance or an audition is learning to play the role. Having read the complete script with a critical eye to grasp the character hints implied in the dialog and stage directions, it is now time for you to translate those hints into an industrious preparation blueprint.

Approach each classroom performance or audition in a calm and relaxed manner. Remember that the teacher or director may have already begun to make assumptions about your monolog character based on his or her own reading of the script. Even the most careful script analysis may not provide the clues necessary to explain why you are not reviewed favorably or even cast in a production. Think of the classroom performance or audition as an opportunity to display a strong stage personality, showcase competitive vocal and physical flexibility, demonstrate script interpretation skills, and exhibit a well-disciplined and mature acting technique.

In learning to play the role, it is a good idea to have a "mental symbol" that helps you to identify and define the monolog character. A mental symbol indicates the character's desire or objective in the monolog, what actions the character is willing to commit to achieve the desire or objective, and the price that must be paid by the character for that desire or objective. Isolating the primary desire or objective in the monolog should stimulate the character's mental symbol and stimulate the character's action and reaction in performance. In giving the monolog character's desire or objective a specific name, you should also be better prepared to express your character's attitude, motivation, or point of view.

Following are some familiar character desires or objectives that may be useful examples to consider. Think of these examples as performance goals in classroom performances or auditions. Define your own character's mental symbol based on your analysis and interpretation of the complete script, as well as the character's primary desire or objective as it is revealed in the selected monolog.

5

Mild Objective	Strong Objective
To force someone to recognize me	To force someone to apologize
To prove my innocence	To get what's owed to me
To get my own reward	To persuade others to my point of view
To force the issue	To force the resolution
To beg forgiveness	To plead for mercy
To teach a lesson	To teach a moral
To end a relationship	To end a friendship
To get what I want	To get what I deserve
To discover the truth	To conceal the truth
To convince others I'm right	To deny I'm wrong

Surface details, familiar actions, incidental events, and spontaneous reactions will all contribute to reveal a character's inner life when the mental symbol has a specific name. Think of your monolog character as a "subject," rather than an "object." Select desires or objectives that are appropriate for the script, call for specific actions to be performed, give added dimension to your interpretation, and are a challenge to perform.

Step Three

The third, and perhaps most important, step in classroom performance or audition is the rehearsal period. The rehearsal period is an excellent time to review your initial analysis and interpretation of the monolog character, discover new insights that surface through improvisation, explore vocal and physical exercises, and polish your acting technique.

This is the time to be open and flexible — vocally and physically — and to fill in any blanks left unanswered about your monolog character's primary desire or objective. Any performance revision, however, should not contradict the basic character outline indicated in your analysis of the complete script.

The rehearsal period is a time to catalog a character's mannerisms, gestures, posture, movement, and vocal qualities suggested in the monolog. It is also a good time to experiment with personal behavior or habits of the character that might give added meaning to the performance. Some actors use the rehearsal period to search for a metaphor, or implied comparison between the character and an unexpected object. Other actors use the rehearsal period to engage in "word play" with lines of dialog to heighten the meaning of selected words or phrases or to punctuate the tempo and rhythm of the language spoken by the character. A few actors use the rehearsal period to visualize images, symbols, or themes suggested in the monolog and then explore inventive strategies to give those images, symbols, or themes more concrete forms of vocal and physical expression.

Regardless of the approach you may take in the rehearsal period, there are some basic principles that should be part of your preparation blueprint. 1) The rehearsal period should be a regularly scheduled practice session that trains the voice and body to respond promptly to any vocal or physical demand suggested in the monolog. 2) The rehearsal period should break down the monolog into a series of character intentions called "beats." A beat begins when a character's intention begins, and ends with its completion. 3) The rehearsal period should allow time to explore subtext, or the hidden meaning of a character's action, attitude, or language.

The rehearsal period should also permit sufficient time to experiment with alternative performance techniques. One popular alternative technique is "objective memory," in which you re-create the basic stimuli present during a past emotional experience or episode and then recall or re-experience the stimuli in an interpretation of a similar experience or episode described by the monolog character. Another very popular alternative technique is "substitution," or transfer, in which you identify a specific person from recent or past life experiences and incorporate selected vocal or physical characteristics, gestures, or mannerisms from that person into your monolog character performance.

It is not enough to rehearse the monolog only for classroom performance or an audition. You should set time aside to write an introduction and transitions for the monolog(s), select props or other theatrical accessories, stage the movement that helps visualize your monolog character's action, practice relaxation exercises, memorize dialog, and pursue a disciplined rehearsal schedule. You should also decide if you wish to videotape the performance for a preliminary assessment of vocal and physical technique or preview the performance before an invited audience of friends or fellow actors. Whether you choose to videotape or preview your monolog performance, the primary goal should be to make appropriate adjustments and to anticipate initial reactions of an audience. Do not, however, seriously compromise what you have discovered, refined, and then polished in either the analysis of the script or in the rehearsal period.

7

The Basic Practices

There are a number of basic practices to be aware of when preparing for classroom performance or an audition. 1) Performances and auditions start on time and monologs are memorized. 2) Performances and auditions that specifically call for a "classical" monolog mean a script written in verse or featuring poetic imagery and language. 3) Performances and auditions are in standard American speech that is free of vocal regionalism, slang, colloquial expressions, and distracting speech or vocal patterns. The use of accents or dialects should be minimal and then only if accurate. 4) Performances and auditions may be limited to three or four minutes for two contrasting monologs. Edit longer excerpts to meet the time limit. 5) Performances and auditions may cause anxiety or nervousness so avoid stimulants like alcohol, caffeine, diet or pep pills, and sugar. Do not chew gum unless it is an essential part of the monolog character portrait.

In selecting a monolog, avoid choosing one from a longer script you have recently performed. Repeating familiar monologs from previous performances may not enhance the self-image you wish to portray in an audition or complement your range of emotional, vocal, and intellectual qualities. You want to achieve a realistic and memorable monolog character portrait in classroom performances or auditions. Any attempt to startle or to exaggerate should also be avoided as a source of distraction. There should also be no theatrical posing, "mugging," or posturing that might contradict the action or character portrait being sketched.

Classroom performances or auditions involve elaborate pre-planning and a disciplined rehearsal schedule. Be meticulous in your studied approach to pre-planning and rehearsal preparation. The "performance sense" you develop in these exercises will provide a working blueprint that frames all your future creative efforts. Now, please familiarize yourself with each of the following special features associated with classroom performance and audition etiquette. Understanding each practice should result in competent and competitive classroom performances and auditions.

Audience

It takes self-confidence to perform solo. Do not lose your concentration if individual members of the audience suddenly look down to write or turn to whisper to each other. They may actually be writing positive comments or sharing favorable opinions. It is not a good idea to focus on a specific individual in the audience to represent the person your monolog character may be addressing. This approach may be very uncomfortable for individual members of the audience, and it may also be distracting for you if the focal person loses interest, becomes self-conscious, or simply stops paying attention to your performance.

Audition Form

The preliminary audition form, or try-out sheet, needs to be filled in completely. It is important to indicate both home and work telephone numbers. Don't forget to list all potential conflicts, work hours, regularly scheduled appointments, classes, or any anticipated obligations that might occur during the announced rehearsal, production, or performance dates. Make mention of any musical instruments played or specialized skills you have, such as sports, magic tricks, gymnastics, foreign languages, tap dance, or impersonations. The audition form is like a job application form, so your responses need to be direct and honest.

Audition Photograph/Resume

Some auditions may request a professional photograph and an acting resume. The professional photograph is generally a current, informal, and natural-pose black-and-white 8" x 10" headshot. The photograph should be well-lit with limited shadowing and should reveal you in an informal, natural pose wearing subtle makeup and a light-colored blouse and having neatly cut hair. Avoid highly theatrical or artificially posed photographs. The acting resume is also 8" x 10" and should be stapled or attached with rubber cement to the back side of the photograph. Information to be included on the resume includes your complete name and current mailing address; home and business phone number; height, weight, and age range; hair and eye color; and singing range. In listing previous acting experience, place the most current credits first and list the name of the character played, title of script, and theatre in which the production was staged.

Callbacks

If callbacks are posted for a final audition performance, materials are usually selected for you. Be prepared, however, for vocal or physical improvisations, cold readings, and, perhaps, a brief interview session. Try not to plan any responses in advance. Do not anticipate the character or the scene that you may be asked to perform. Be attentive to the callback order of scheduled final auditions. Know who you follow so that last-minute routines such as relaxation exercises or last-minute emergencies such as a missing button or a restroom break will not delay your final call or disrupt your concentration.

Climax

Audition monologs that are performed out of context from a longer script do not always have a structure that indicates beginning, middle, and end. As part of the rehearsal period, you need to make a clear choice about the climax of the monolog in performance. The climax should be the moment of highest tension, and usually comes toward the end of the middle section or at the end section of the monolog. Making a specific choice of the climactic moment should build suspense and indicate a forward performance momentum that is resolved at last in a memorable moment. When you identify the climactic moment, keep in mind that it should be fairly short or it will lose significance.

Entrance

Your initial entrance is an integral part of the audition and should be handled with poise. As soon as you enter, seize the space! Walk with self-confidence and make direct eye contact with the audience. If you need to move a chair or set up the space, do so quickly and quietly. Then go directly to the spot from which you have chosen to introduce yourself. Look at the audience and decide where you will focus the monolog. Your introduction should be brief and delivered in the center stage space. Don't forget to pause before and after your introduction. Do not chat, shake hands, or approach the audience after the audition.

Exit

At the end of your audition, pause to hold the climactic moment of the monolog and then make eye contact with the audience. Simply say, "Thank you" and exit the space with the same poise that marked your entrance. Don't forget to keep your head up as you exit! There is no need to comment on your performance — especially to offer hasty apologies or make excuses. Be prepared if you are asked to do a cold reading or improvisation or respond to interview questions following the audition. Rehearse the exit until you can consistently sustain the climactic moment of the monolog and leave the space with graceful self-confidence.

Going Up!

Try not to be concerned about "going up," or forgetting your lines, during an audition. You should be prepared through the rigor of the rehearsal period to improvise or paraphrase the monolog. You are the only person with a complete copy of the monolog. Learn to go on as if any hesitation or momentary lapse were just a thoughtful pause that is part of your performance. Of course, you can reduce the possibility of hesitations or lapses in your performance through regularly scheduled reading rehearsals that focus on good memorization skills and line repetition exercises. It is always a good idea to practice your dialog aloud rather than silently in the rehearsal period when memorizing character lines.

Introduction

One of the first steps in pre-planning an audition blueprint is to introduce yourself and the monolog(s) you are performing. The introduction is your first vocal moment on stage and should be marked with a personal signature of self-confidence. The spoken introduction, delivered without notes, should be brief and cordial. A typical introduction might say, "Hello. My name is Rebecca Gerber. I will be doing Linda's "funeral oration" from Arthur Miller's *Death of a Salesman* and Anna's "toilet seat" speech from Paula Vogel's *The Baltimore Waltz*." Introduce both of your monologs at the beginning of the audition so you won't have to come back as "yourself" in the middle of the performance to introduce a second monolog. Don't forget to pause between the end of the introduction and the beginning of the transition that sets the scene for the first monolog.

Makeup

Light street makeup is appropriate for a woman to wear in an audition. Some women wear their hair up for classical monologs, but always away from the face so expressions may be seen clearly. If you have long hair, pull it back so it doesn't fall in your face while performing! Do not rely on excessive makeup, false hair or wigs, hair extensions, padding, or prosthetic devices to flesh-out your monolog character. Accessories like costume jewelry, headbands, multiple bracelets, or feathers should be eliminated. Also avoid wearing platform shoes, knee boots, flip-flops, sandals, or high heels, which tend to make movement awkward or unnatural.

Movement

Movement is less likely to have an immediate impact on an audition than it might have in the performance of a full-length script. Expressive monolog character movement, however, is an audition expectation. Explore subtle movement opportunities that help to define the monolog character in terms of gesture, mannerisms, posture, or stance. Character intention, for example, can be subtly revealed by the way in which a character sits, stands, or walks. Unless you have a specific reason to do otherwise, character movement should progress downstage rather than upstage and away from the audience. If movement includes pacing from side to side, remember to keep your head up and maintain eye contact with the audience! A good rule of thumb is to maintain a balance between movement that helps to visualize character *action* and movement that adds variety to the *tempo* of your performance.

Props

Props should be limited to those specific hand-held objects that are an extension of the monolog character. If you choose to use a prop, it should be indicated in the script and small enough to be handled easily (such as a letter, a fan, glasses, or a photograph kept in your pocket). Do not litter the playing space with an assortment of miscellaneous props that later become part of the performance. A performance is never about props or other theatrical accessories. It is about *you* and how you fill an empty space using yourself as a prop!

Space

Try to visit the space before a scheduled audition. Pay particular attention to the size, entrance and exit doorways, seating arrangement, and acoustics. If possible, rehearse in the space before an audition to discover the vocal and physical demands of the playing area. Familiarity with the space should help promote a more comfortable and relaxed atmosphere in which to execute fluid, natural movement and promote a pleasing vocal quality in performance. Rehearsal in the space should also help to combat the initial anxiety and tension frequently associated with performing in an unfamiliar environment.

Staging

The only furniture you will probably have available to you in an audition is a chair and table. It is not necessary to use assorted benches, beds, desks, sofas, or other elaborate set pieces in staging the monolog. What is important is "placement" in the space. Set up the playing area so you are facing the audience; but place your monolog character at a smart angle downstage. Be careful not to deliver the entire monolog in profile. Look for opportunities to address the audience directly, full front. Unless the monolog suggests otherwise, stage the monolog in the upstage center, center, or upstage right position and move downstage or left/right as action in the monolog suggests. Backing up or even abruptly turning and moving upstage may indicate that you are retreating or starting over. Climaxes appear to be more effective if they are played center stage or downstage center. Remember that excessive or repetitive movement may be distracting in a brief three- or four-minute audition, so work with the minimum movement needed to tell the character's story directly and simply.

Time

Plan to arrive early for an audition — and never arrive late! The scheduled audition time is an appointment and you must be punctual. You can review your monolog(s) or warm up with vocal, physical, or relaxation exercises while waiting for your name to be called. Avoid the tendency to socialize at an audition, and show respect for fellow actors by keeping conversation and noise at a low level. Time also refers to the minutes allocated for an individual audition — usually three to four minutes for two contrasting monologs — so respect those time limits as well. As you rehearse, remember to time your monolog(s) and make appropriate cuts to meet the announced time limit.

Transition(s)

After you have decided on the order in which you will perform your monologs, use brief transitions to move easily from one to the other. Of course, if you are only performing one monolog then there is only one transition necessary to set the scene. Transitional narratives should be memorized and rehearsed as part of the preparation for an audition. Generally, transitions include brief remarks that identify character, locale, and situation.

A transition for a monolog from Christopher Durang's *Death Comes to Us All*, Mary Agnes might, for example, include the following narrative: "Margot Pommes, one of the tempestuous eccentrics living in her family's decaying mansion, suffers from a series of frightful dreams that may reveal dark, unexplained household secrets. She now turns reluctantly to her father for answers."

Wardrobe

An appropriate audition wardrobe subtly reflects the attitude or mood of the monolog character. The wardrobe should be carefully selected in terms of cut, style, and color. Focus on basic designer wardrobe principles of line, color, texture, and simple ornament. Avoid the tendency to wear theatrical costumes or elaborate accessories to an audition. Do not, for example, wear a seventeenth-century style brocade bodice and bustle just because you are playing the chaste Isabella in Shakespeare's *Measure for Measure*. If you are performing two contrasting monologs, dress in a neutral color and allow the actions performed to distinguish the two characters. Wear comfortable clothes and stable shoes that permit easy, fluid movement. Avoid tight jeans, plunging necklines, and short skirts. A subtle, well-chosen audition wardrobe can also reveal a monolog character's lifestyle, occupation, idiosyncrasies, or sense of self.

Warm-Up

Arrive at an audition at least forty-five minutes in advance to warm up your voice and body. A popular audition warm-up is to relax by lying flat on your back and breathing deeply. Place your hand just above your waistline and begin to inhale slowly and then exhale. Notice how the abdominal wall moves in and out as your breathing is controlled and rhythmic. After several minutes, stand up and repeat the exercise. Keep your hand at your waist to detect any change in your center of breathing. Now recite some of your favorite song lyrics or familiar jingles. Encourage your diaphragm to regularly expand and then contract with a comfortable rhythm. Concentrate on keeping your upper chest from rising and falling. Repeat this exercise for short periods of two to three minutes and the relaxation results should be noticeable!

Additional Dimensions

There are a number of additional dimensions to consider in preparing for a classroom performance or audition. First, maintain a current repertoire of two or three monologs or scenes that are appropriate for any type of performance or audition. Your treasure chest of familiar scripts should suit your age and type, demonstrate vocal and physical flexibility, promote ease of movement, and display an intellectual and emotional understanding of character. Second, look for the "acting edition" of a script because it includes italicized stage directions and parenthetical clues that could influence your style of movement or phrasing in character interpretation. Third, when analyzing the piece, use a dictionary to paraphrase your monolog into conversational words that reduce character actions, ideas, and thoughts to one-word adverbs or verbs. Don't forget to "play" the adverbs or verbs in the rehearsal period!

Learn to isolate images, symbols, and evocative language that give a character's dialog its meaning or subtext. This is what the master Russian acting theorist Stanislavski termed discovering the "diction" of a character's spoken and unspoken words. It may also be useful to invent a brief biography that defines a character's interaction and interpersonal relationship with other characters. A character biography personalizes the monolog. It should help you to understand the character's actions, thoughts, and relationships more easily. Finally, find your own "inner space" in the rehearsal period. It could be a deserted island, mountain top, or clearing in the forest — a secluded space where you can feel at peace with yourself and where your dramatic imagination is free to wander.

As part of your performance blueprint, remember to place set pieces, such as a chair or table, down right or down left stage so the center of the playing space is open to frame character movement. Locate any imaginary character(s) in the audience and slightly above the heads of the viewers. Rehearse in a number of different spaces to anticipate auditions that might be held in a studio, community center, tent, cafeteria, gymnasium, classroom, or traditional theatre.

If the monolog character must speak with a dialect, cultivate a catalog of performance accents. The primary performance accents — British, Cockney, German, Italian, New York (Brooklyn), Southern American, Spanish, Oriental, Gypsy, and Midwestern — may be voiced with accuracy if you learn the phonetic alphabet. Purchasing accent tapes, listening to radio or television ethnic characters speak, or viewing foreign film clips is also a good rehearsal strategy. Don't forget to practice your character accent in everyday conversation as well, whether informally with friends or more formally at a shopping mall that features a variety of multicultural cafes or restaurants.

At this point you should have a good sense of the basic classroom performance and audition principles. It is now time to review the monolog characters you might select for further study. These are very distinct character voices. They speak from their own observations and are shaped by their own lived experiences. You will discover that these flesh-and-blood characters are authentic people who live everyday life with a sense of personal dignity. Become attuned to their gentle humor, emphatic protests, or impassioned pleas and you will experience a genuine response that will leave a memorable imprint on your classroom performance or audition.

Chapter II

The Age of Innocence

Bitter are the tears of a child:
  Sweeten them.
Deep are the thoughts of a child:
  Quiet them.
Sharp is the grief of a child:
  Take it from her.
Soft is the heart of a child:
  Do not harden it.

— *Pamela Glenconner,* A Child

The monolog characters in this chapter are not all youthful adolescents innocently engaged in childish role-playing games. Some are mature and strong-willed adults who still cling to their youthful innocence and childhood memories as a convenient escape from the grim and sober reality of the adult world in which they now live. Their collective stories chronicle personal testimonies of highly sensitive personal and private issues that speak more to a sense of anguish and frustration than a state of innocence. When you probe beneath the surface of their fictional lives, however, you will be surprised to discover an internal struggle to confront impending adulthood and the awakening of repressed desires or hidden passions in these irrepressible characters.

The age of innocence describes a wider range of life experience than you may suspect at first glance. There is a sense of urgency in these characters. Their awkwardness or insecurity in trying to express personal despair or sadness may result in some abrupt shifts in attitude or mood as they voice bold new themes. The monolog characters are free-spirited, reckless, and sometimes uninhibited in their behavior. This will lend an added dimension of risk-taking in classroom performances or auditions.

In playing these monologs you will need to capture the indescribable "life spirit" of characters who are spontaneous and unpredictable. You will also have to weave a texture of directness and simplicity into the performance to call immediate attention to the passion that lurks beneath the surface of each character's personal story. It may be difficult at first to imagine yourself as some of these stage figures. It is important, therefore, to focus on the character's physicality, especially her mannerisms or personal habits, to help clarify basic impulses or sudden outbursts. Taking this approach to performance should reveal new layers of subtext and subtle shades of undercurrent meaning in the spoken and unspoken dialog.

Dreams of Anne Frank
by Bernard Kops

1 Anne   Youthful/Teen

2

3 *This excerpt is based on the real-life story of the extraordinary*
4 *thirteen-year-old Jewish girl who went into hiding with her*
5 *family after the Nazi occupation of Holland* (Diary of Anne
6 Frank). *The retelling of that story is an imaginative exploration of*
7 *Anne's fanciful thoughts and dreams. Through these she can*
8 *escape, travel, prophesy, and even change the course of history.*

9

10 *(Holding up a yellow star.)* **Morning star. Evening star.**
11 **Yellow star. Amsterdam. Nineteen forty-two. The German**
12 **army occupies Holland. They have applied terrible rules that**
13 **we must obey. Rules for Jews. That applies to me. 'Jews**
14 **must wear a yellow star. Jews cannot go on trains. Jews**
15 **must not drive. Jews cannot go shopping, except between**
16 **three and five. Jews must only patronize Jewish shops.' We**
17 **cannot go to the cinema, play tennis, go swimming. I cannot**
18 **even go to the theatre. And now for the most frightening**
19 **thing of all. They are beginning to round Jews up and take**
20 **us away. Away from our homes, our beloved Amsterdam. A**
21 **few days ago I celebrated my thirteenth birthday. My**
22 **parents gave me this diary. It is my most precious**
23 **possession. Yesterday I was just an ordinary girl living in**
24 **Amsterdam. Today I am forced to wear this by our Nazi**
25 **conquerors. Morning star, evening star, yellow star.**
26   **It was Sunday. The fifth of July. The day after American**
27 **Independence Day. My mother pretended she wasn't crying.**
28   **Then Father made the announcement. I remember his**
29 **exact words. 'Listen, children. Please. I must tell you**

1 something. We're going into hiding.' When are we going into
2 hiding? Will we be alright? What do I leave behind? What can
3 I take? *(Getting her satchel.)* **Essentials. My school satchel. I'm**
4 **going to cram it full. Hair curlers. Handkerchiefs. School**
5 **books. Film star photographs. Joan Crawford. Bette Davis.**
6 **Deanna Durbin. Mickey Rooney. Comb. Letters. Thousands of**
7 **pencils. Elastic bands. My best book.** *Emil and the Detectives.*
8 **Five pens.** *(She smells a little bottle.)* **Nice scent. Oh, yes!**
9 **Mustn't forget my new diary.** *(She has put all her things into her*
10 *satchel but she has not included her diary.)* **We're going into**
11 **hiding. Going into hiding.**
12 Four days later. It was Thursday, the ninth of July. I shall
13 never forget that morning. It was raining. Imagine leaving your
14 house, maybe for ever.
15 I'm so happy. In hiding we no longer have to obey the
16 Germans, the master race. No more dreaded rules for Jews.
17 Goodbye, House. We'll always remember you. Thank you for
18 everything. My brain is at a fairground, on the roller coaster.
19 Up and down. Happy. Sad. Afraid. Excited. My emotions are
20 racing. My imagination spilling over. After all, I am a creative
21 artist. I'm going to be a writer when this war is over.
22 Diary! Can't go without my diary. *(She takes up the diary*
23 *and opens it.)* **You can be trapped in a box, or in sadness, but**
24 **you travel in your mind. You can be imprisoned in a basement**
25 **or an attic, but you can go anywhere. In your dreams you are**
26 **free, the past, the present, the future. It is all open to you**
27 **within my pages. Use me well.** *(As herself.)* **I promise. I shall**
28 **write everything down. Everything. Thoughts. Events. Dreams.**
29 **I shall confide my secrets. Only to you.** *(Clutching her diary*
30 *close.)* **Let's go. My diary. I couldn't survive without my diary.**
31
32
33
34
35

driver's ed.
by Steven A. Schutzman

1   Patricia   Teen

2

3   *Patricia, a troubled teenager still coping with the recent death of*
4   *her father, is very anxious to be taking her first driving lesson.*
5   *Although she is bright, perky, and mature for her age, Patricia*
6   *has unsettled issues to address. Although intent on impressing*
7   *the teacher she admires, much more surfaces here as the teenager*
8   *recalls her father's tragic death and offers a glimpse of recent*
9   *family events.*

10

11   I have the highest grade point average in my class. I
12 make my own clothes and could play the flute
13 professionally. It's something to fall back on, my mother
14 says. I also sing and dance. Last year I was the star of the
15 school musical. I have never failed at anything. All the boys
16 are idiots. When I sleep down in the basement, I can hear
17 my mother and her boyfriend Donny through the air
18 conditioner ducts. Donny has a silver Jaguar. He let me
19 drive it once in the parking lot of the old fairgrounds. My
20 mother waited only seven months before she'd let Donny
21 sleep over. Do you think that's enough time? I don't.
22   After my father died, I used to see his ghost sitting on
23 my windowsill and his ghost seemed happy, and that made
24 me happy. Ghosts can't talk and they can't hear you talk.
25 It's not like Hamlet at all. Ghosts just want to be in the
26 room with you. They just want you to see them. I filled a
27 whole composition book the night I first saw Dad again. My
28 hand couldn't stop. Whenever I read it over it makes me cry.
29 I will be reading it over my whole life. 'Let me introduce you

1   to who I was and let who I am now express the terrible
2   surprise of what has happened to me.' How could a twelve-
3   year-old write that?
4   I'm a virgin. I have my father's eyes. For more than a year
5   afterward, every night at six o'clock the dog would sit by the
6   door and wait for Dad. My brother, who's in college now,
7   thought it was the sequence of cars coming home to the
8   neighborhood; every car but Dad's, so it fooled the dog. The
9   dog has lived in that house all his life and so have I. He will
10 be famous one day, my brother not the dog.
11   I started sleeping in the basement when my mother
12 started letting Donny stay over, for privacy, but when their
13 lovemaking noises come through the ducts I can't help but
14 listen. If I asked, would you kiss me just once?
15
16
17
18
19
20
21
22
23
24
25
26
27
28
29
30
31
32
33
34
35

A Thirteen-Year-Old Maid
by Anne Thackeray
edited by Lydia Cosentino

1 Maid   Youthful/Teen
2
3 *This 1874 historical document offers a fragile account of an*
4 *unnamed thirteen-year-old maid at work in mid-nineteenth*
5 *century England. It is an intimate glimpse of the daily life and idle*
6 *chatter of a "clever, stumpy little thing" who has a good helping*
7 *of strength, will, and spirit to sustain her labors. There is a slight*
8 *Cockney accent possible in the maid's dialog that should lend an*
9 *air of authenticity to the character.*
10
11   Oh, I've been a servant for years! I learnt ironing off the
12 lady. I didn't know nothing about it. I didn't know nothing
13 about anything. I didn't know where to buy the wood for the
14 fire. I run along the street and asked the first person I saw
15 where the woodshop was. I was frightened — oh, I was.
16   They wasn't particular kind in my first place. I had
17 plenty to eat — it wasn't anything of that. They jest give me
18 an egg, and they says, 'There, get your dinner,' but not
19 anything more. I had to do all the work. I'd no one to go to.
20 Oh! I cried the first night. I used to cry so. I had always slep
21 in a ward full of other girls, and there I was all alone, and
22 this was a great big house — Oh, so big! And they told me
23 to go downstairs, in a room by the kitchen all alone, with a
24 long black passage. I might have screamed, but nobody
25 would have heard. An archtec, the gen'l'man was. I got to
26 break everything. Oh, I was frightened!
27   Then I got a place in a family where there was nine
28 children. I was about fourteen then. I earned two shillings a

1 week. I used to get up and light the fire, bathe them and then
2 dress them, and git their breakfasts, and the lady sometimes
3 would go up to London on business, and then I had the baby,
4 too, and it couldn't be left, and had to be fed. I'd take them
5 all out for a walk on the common. There was one, a cripple.
6 She couldn't walk about.
7   Then there was dinner, and to wash up after; and then by
8 that time it would be tea-time again. And then I had to put the
9 nine children to bed and bathe them, and clean up the rooms
10 and fires at night. There was no time in the morning. And then
11 there would be the gen'l'man's supper to get.
12   Oh! That was a hard place. I wasn't in bed till twelve, and
13 I'd be up by six. I stopped there nine months. I hadn't no one
14 to help me. Oh, yes, I had — the baker. He told me of another
15 place. I've been there three year. I'm cook, and they are very
16 kind, but I tell the girls there's none of 'em had such work as
17 me. I'm very fond of reading, but I ain't no time for reading!
18
19
20
21
22
23
24
25
26
27
28
29
30
31
32
33
34
35

The Wonderbread Passion
by Christopher Woods

1 Maria   Young Adult

2

3 *In this darkly unsettling comic excerpt, a lonely young woman*
4 *quietly reflects on her early failures in love in a plaintive cry for*
5 *help. As she unearths painful, personal memories and private*
6 *confessions, there is a fragility and basic humanity that emerges*
7 *to paint the portrait of a sadder but, hopefully, wiser young*
8 *woman who is all too aware of her own limitations and liabilities.*

9

10 I've known pain, personally. On the night of my senior
11 prom, my date didn't show up. He was to come at seven
12 o'clock. At seven-forty, my father told me the boy wasn't
13 coming. At seven-forty-five, my mother made me take off
14 my dress. She said it would wrinkle. Or that it might stain
15 because of my tears. Then, at nine o'clock, my father
16 offered to take me to the prom himself. But I said no.
17 *(Chokes back tears.)* By then, it didn't matter. Later on, I
18 found out that my date had taken another boy to the prom.
19 Something about minority rights. To be honest, I never
20 understood it. Wasn't I alone? Wasn't I the smallest minority
21 of all? To this day, my prom gown is packed in mothballs.
22 It hurts to talk about it even now.

23 I decided that I had to get beyond my prom. Oh, it took
24 a few years, but I got over it. I decided to become a candy
25 striper at the hospital. If I took care of people with serious
26 problems, maybe I could forget my own. Oh, I know some
27 people think a candy striper is nothing more than a bedpan
28 carrier. But I assure you, it is much, much more. Maybe not
29 the most important job in a hospital but a necessary one.

1   I wanted to do good. And no matter what my superior
2   thought, I know I was good. In orientation, they said the most
3   important thing a candy striper could do was to smile. I took
4   it to heart. I always smiled. I have to tell you, it wasn't always
5   easy. Why, when a patient dies, it's very difficult to keep
6   smiling. But I did. That's when the complaints started. I tried
7   to explain why I kept smiling, but my superior called me an
8   idiot. And then she fired me. From a volunteer job!
9   I will never be the same. And, to tell you the truth, I don't
10   smile so much anymore.
11
12
13
14
15
16
17
18
19
20
21
22
23
24
25
26
27
28
29
30
31
32
33
34
35

Backwater
by Leon Kaye

1	Annie	Young Adult

2

3 *Annie, a twenty-three-year-old college student studying*
4 *molecular biology, is back home in Mississippi to visit her*
5 *brother, a local sheriff. Barefoot and dressed as a backwoods*
6 *Southerner for the annual "Huckleberry Finn" parade, Annie*
7 *overhears a Chicago writer, Briggs, making disparaging remarks*
8 *about the locals and decides to have some fun with him by*
9 *concocting a hilarious story to introduce herself.*

10

11   Most people in these parts like to marry in the family.
12 That's 'cause they're usually drunk and travel is difficult
13 when you have difficulty walkin'. But nobody likes me 'round
14 here 'cause I'm different. My family had one of those mixed
15 marriages. *(Whispering.)* My grandfather was a 'coon. *(Briggs*
16 *leans on the desk, crosses arms, and looks down at the floor.)*
17   You're uncomfortable. You think I'm talkin' 'bout a colored
18 fellow. No, siree. What I mean is my grandfather was a
19 raccoon is what he was. *(Briggs laughs.)* You don't believe me.
20 Why do you think I've got these big dark circles under my
21 eyes? *(He laughs louder.)* Yup. My daddy was one-half Irish.
22 But you couldn't tell much by lookin' at him. He was pretty
23 normal, normal height and all. And his mamma never
24 broadcast it. But everyone knew he was part 'coon 'cause my
25 daddy liked to go out at night and rummage through the
26 garbage. That and he had these funny lookin' rodent teeth.
27 Nobody could whittle through a two-by-four like daddy. *(Briggs*
28 *leans back on the desk, soaks in her tall tale.)*
29   And my daddy loved me. There was no one my daddy

1 loved more, 'cept for his Ford pickup. But he had to give that
2 up 'cause there was a town ordinance about not keepin' rusty
3 pieces of junk in front of your house. So he had to get it
4 towed. But he loved that truck. He even kept some engine and
5 exhaust parts for senty-mental value. He loved those parts,
6 kept them in his room right next to his bed on top of a photo
7 of momma and George Wallace. And he used to sing to the
8 parts every night before he went out. *(Singing.)* 'Have faith,
9 hope and charity. That's the way to live successfully.'
10   *(Sadly.)* I would hear him singin', and I got jealous. So I
11 went one night when daddy was out at a pig-wrestlin' match,
12 and I swiped his catalytic converter and his distributor cap. I
13 buried them out back right next to my dog Clyde. The first dog
14 Clyde, not the second dog Clyde. And I sat in my bedroom,
15 just waitin' and listenin' for him to come in. He came home
16 and right away he knew somethin' was up. He would always
17 grind his two big rodent teeth together when he knew
18 somethin' was up. And immediately I regretted what I had
19 done. I was about to get up and tell him but then I heard my
20 daddy's voice. He was yellin', 'Someone touched my private
21 parts! Someone touched my private parts!' He was like a
22 crazy person. And just dumb luck, there was two police
23 officers and the head of our church walking by. They came
24 rushin' in, pushed my daddy to the floor, and took him away
25 in handcuffs. And that was the last I ever saw of him!
26
27
28
29
30
31
32
33
34
35

A Blue Streak
by Staci Swedeen

1 Sarah Sue   Youthful
2
3 *Here is a comic juvenile character role that presents an opportunity*
4 *for the performer to play a musical instrument. Sarah Sue, a mature*
5 *fifth-grader, has marching orders from her parents to round out her*
6 *education by joining the school band. Sarah Sue's choice of*
7 *instrument is the tuba, but she soon changes her mind when she*
8 *discovers a new interest in her life. (Music inserts are indicated for*
9 *performers who may wish to include an instrument in the*
10 *performance.)*
11
12   My name is Sarah Sue Perkins and I am in the fifth grade.
13 I hate the fifth grade. It's filled with stupid boys like Alfred
14 Brewster and Sammy Buchwald, who threw spit balls at me
15 all last year. I liked Sammy up until then. Now they think
16 telling a fart joke is the funniest thing in the world. Ha, ha. I
17 hate the fifth grade because our teacher, Mrs. Boynton, has
18 actually told us — out loud — that after teaching school for
19 three years she is never having children. Like that's our fault
20 or something. And I hate the fifth grade because my parents
21 have told me I have to join band. *(Music insert.)*
22   I don't know why. My brother Timmy plays trumpet. My
23 sister Lisa plays piano. That should be enough music for any
24 family, but noooo. My father used to play in a band in 'the
25 good old days,' which means before he got married. He says
26 that our education will not be complete without a 'musical
27 component.' He likes to use words like 'component,' 'full
28 spectrum,' 'holistic,' and 'digital.' He likes to say that some
29 things change and some things stay the same; and that the

1 most important thing in life is learning how to learn. Timmy,
2 Lisa, and I try to humor him, but secretly we think he's kind of
3 nuts. Besides, my education will be complete any day now —
4 after I drop out of fifth grade. Don't tell my parents though,
5 okay? My mother has repeatedly told me to stop testing her
6 limits, and I'm pretty sure this will. *(Music insert.)*
7   Today we went down to the school to look over instruments.
8 Both of my parents came with me and even though they said
9 they wouldn't try to influence my selection, they just couldn't
10 help themselves. 'How about the tuba?' I asked. 'Or the French
11 horn? Or the drums?' I want something so big and splashy that
12 when I blow into it the world will explode — something
13 awesome and amazing. Something that will lift the house up
14 and throw it into the air. 'Can I Dad? Huh?' And Dad would go,
15 'Now Sarah Sue, that's an interesting choice' and Mom would
16 let out a little whistle from between her lips and they'd wander
17 a little ways ahead of me. Then Daddy came to the aisle with
18 the clarinets. *(Music insert.)*
19   'Sarah Sue, this looks like your instrument,' Daddy said.
20 The clarinet? Who wants to play the clarinet! I could only look
21 at him. Like, what kind of father forces his daughter to play a
22 little black stick when she wants to play the tuba? I stood there
23 considering killing myself when Sammy Buchwald and his dad
24 came up to the clarinet section too. Sammy gave me a kind of
25 goofy grin and said, 'Hey, Sarah Sue, looks like we're both
26 going to be in the same section of the band.' I ignored him.
27 'Sarah Sue,' he went on, 'listen … about those spit balls.'
28 'What?' I said. He motioned to me to step away from our
29 parents, and I did though I acted like I didn't want to. 'What?'
30 'Alfred only threw them at you because he likes you.' 'Really?'
31 I said. 'What about you? Why did you throw them, then?' He
32 turned all red and ran away, which made me go … mmmm. I
33 walked back over to where my Dad was standing. 'So honey,'
34 Dad said. 'How do you feel about getting this clarinet?' 'Daddy,'
35 I said, 'I wouldn't think of playing anything else!'

Why Is John Lennon Wearing a Skirt?
by Claire Dowie

1   Young Woman   Adult
2
3   *This excerpt from a long-running British one-woman show is*
4   *about rekindling the passion of being female. It follows the life*
5   *and experiences of one young woman who doesn't want to be a*
6   *"girl" and chooses to pursue her own lifestyle without conforming*
7   *to stereotypes of "womanly" behavior. In this episode, having*
8   *fantasized about her ideal experience of the Women's Liberation*
9   *movement, the young woman attends her first meeting.*
10
11   Then I went to a meeting. A women only group. I said,
12   'Who's in charge?' and they said, 'We all are.' And they
13   talked about sisterhood and patriarchy and politics — or
14   more to the point, how they hated men. And I said, 'Doesn't
15   anybody hate women? Doesn't anybody hate being a
16   woman? Doesn't anybody hate being thought of as kind and
17   gentle and understanding and supportive and patient and
18   democratic and nurturing and reasonable and non-
19   aggressive and helpful and self-sacrificing and fair-minded
20   and co-operative? Doesn't anybody hate being thought of as
21   nice? Like a biscuit? Doesn't anybody want to be a hero?
22   Doesn't anybody just love what men do and want to do it
23   too? Isn't there anybody here who's insanely jealous that
24   they weren't born a boy? That they weren't born with the
25   opportunity to do anything they wanted to do without having
26   to apologize or justify or explain or feel guilty or awkward or
27   feel like a freak or be ridiculed or persecuted or ostracized
28   or wait till it's fashionable?' And they said, 'No.' And I said,
29   'What's wrong with me then, why am I such a freak? Why

1   can't I just be a woman? What are you then?' And they said,
2   'Oppressed.' Fine. Be that then.
3
4
5
6
7
8
9
10
11
12
13
14
15
16
17
18
19
20
21
22
23
24
25
26
27
28
29
30
31
32
33
34
35

Hope Throws Her Heart Away
by Susan Goodell

1 Office Worker   Young Adult

2

3 *A young, beleaguered clerk working in a small office for an*
4 *unseen employer is desperately trying to survive her numbing*
5 *job. The action here has some amusing moments, but is primarily*
6 *routine office business that takes a serious turn when the office*
7 *worker realizes that her spirit is so deadened she cannot escape*
8 *this "glamour job."*

9

10 Work is not the glamorous life I planned for myself. When
11 you say 'work,' my first word association is panty hose. You
12 have to wake up. You have to be here all day. Five days out
13 of seven days, you sit, right here. They give you a chair with
14 a lot of padding. They want you to sit a long time. The
15 longer you sit, the more they like it. Some people are here
16 years. They look all right. I once planned to be a ballerina.
17 I couldn't dance. I wanted to wear the tutu. You gotta find
18 things to do all day. Opening the desk drawer and closing
19 it. That's an activity. Checking everything in the drawer.
20 Making sure your paper clip box isn't empty. Flipping the
21 paper clip over ... and over ... and over.
22 I like having something I can feel. Finding a reason to
23 get up from your desk so you can walk in the hall. Walking
24 helps me stay awake. Though it's better if I'm not in the hall
25 too much. It looks like I'm not working. People notice you
26 more if they always see you walking back and forth, back
27 and forth, drinking water, getting supplies, going to the
28 ladies room, back and forth. They start wondering if you're
29 working. It's O.K. to be at my desk. At least I can think

1 about anything I want, as long as it looks like I'm thinking
2 about work.
3   You spend about twenty-five percent of your life in the
4 office. But when you count lunch hour, which you would do
5 completely differently if you weren't at the office, getting ready
6 to go to the office, going to the office, going home from the
7 office, and forgetting the office, it's most of your life. I decide
8 what I'll eat for lunch early. Then I can think about it all
9 morning. I should eat less. My stomach looks like an
10 accordion. I once was going to be a train engineer. The same
11 time I was going to be a ballerina. I never questioned how I
12 would do both. I wait the whole day for time to leave. I wait
13 the whole week for the weekend. I wait the whole year for
14 vacation. But when it finally comes, I don't go anywhere. I
15 can't decide where to go.
16
17
18
19
20
21
22
23
24
25
26
27
28
29
30
31
32
33
34
35

My Lost State
by Flannery Fager

1 Easter	Teen/Young Adult

2

3 *Sixteen-year-old Easter recounts an extraordinary experience that*
4 *defies logical and sensible conclusions, but ultimately changes her*
5 *life. She takes her listeners along, step-by-step, on this strange*
6 *journey and conveys her deep sense of separation from the world*
7 *and from herself. This mysterious story asks us to think about the*
8 *essential inconsistency of reality and absurdity of life.*

9

10 I didn't realize how much power I had until I saw myself
11 in the mirror — the mirror in the bathroom of the home where
12 I lived when I was eleven years old. The thing is, I was sixteen
13 by then and living in Tampa, Florida, about a thousand miles
14 away. Unmistakably, though, that was my face, my current
15 face with its recently added emerald nose stud, reflected in
16 the downstairs bathroom mirror at 471 Monarch Street,
17 Richmond, Indiana.
18   I studied the rest of the wall as it came into focus. The
19 new owners hadn't bothered to replace the crimson-foil
20 wallpaper my mom had hated. I used to secretly like the
21 tacky, almost Christmassy way it brightened the windowless
22 room. Now it just looked shabby, as if the kids who came
23 after me had taken turns trying to peel the paper from a once
24 invisible seam. 'What is this,' I wondered. 'A dream? A
25 hallucination? A memory twisted by wishful thinking?' I
26 blinked twice but remained inexplicably incarnated in my
27 family's former bathroom. I studied my hands. All jewelry
28 accounted for, including my most recent pewter armor ring,
29 Jess's parting gift before my latest move, from Atlanta to

1 Tampa. Not much mental math required to grasp that the house
2 I was involuntarily revisiting was already five homes ago. Five
3 increasingly unhappy homes ago.
4   Footsteps from the hall jolted me into near panic. How
5 could I explain to a stranger what I couldn't begin to explain to
6 myself? 'Hi. You don't know me, but I used to live here. Don't
7 worry. I don't have a key. Or a clue how I got here from Florida.
8 Last thing I knew I was in third period French conjugating the
9 verb *venir*.' The door, already ajar, swung toward me. I tensed
10 for the inevitable screech of fright. Women scream. Men gasp or
11 yelp. Or simply strike in self-defense. Somewhere in the house
12 a phone rang. The door froze in mid-swing. A voice on the other
13 side cried, 'If that's for me, I'm gone!' It was an oddly throaty
14 voice, more like a loud purr than a shout. Before I could imagine
15 its source, the door opened the rest of the way, and in stepped
16 a stocky blonde about twenty years old. The bathroom was tiny.
17 I had no room to move.
18   'I'm harmless!' I declared before the blonde could react. But
19 the blonde didn't react. She didn't seem to notice me. She just
20 peered into the mirror, tilting her head from side to side, fluffing
21 her already tousled hair. I stared as our reflections overlapped.
22 The blonde was standing where I was standing. We were in
23 precisely the same place at precisely the same time. Or were
24 we? Our faces blurred and separated and blurred again. 'That
25 was Angie!' a man's voice thundered. 'She's got the flu.' The
26 blonde stopped primping. She stared at her reflection — at
27 what I saw as our combined reflections — so intently that I
28 stiffened again. Then the blonde smiled. In her furry little voice,
29 she muttered, 'Angie should wish she's got the flu.' To the man
30 somewhere in the house where I used to live, she shouted,
31 'That's too bad. I'll go check on her.'
32   Then the blonde was gone, and I was back in French class
33 at Fowler High, where I began to understand that the problem I
34 had been wrestling with an hour before probably wasn't my
35 biggest problem after all.

Between Stars
by Matthew Wilkie

1   Cameron   Adult

2

3   *Cameron, the only female astronaut on board the Jeunet, is orbiting*
4   *the Earth with her comrades when the capsule is seriously*
5   *damaged in a meteor storm. An attempt at external repair work*
6   *fails, leaving the voyagers stranded in space. As the astronauts*
7   *retreat into their separate cubicles to contemplate the inevitable,*
8   *Cameron recalls a prophetic conversation with her mother.*

9

10   When I was outside, I remembered something.
11   Something I had once been told. *(Pause)* It was like a
12   fireworks on bonfire night ... a rocket out of control.
13   Screams and wails in every direction. Children not sure
14   whether to laugh or run for cover. The rocket finally fading
15   out of sight. *(Pause)*
16   At the time, it meant little to me. It wasn't until later
17   that — I think — I think I started to understand. *(Pause)*
18   Before I left, my mother came up to me — told me about
19   how she remembered watching the television as a child.
20   Watching a shuttle launch into space. One of the first. Seven
21   people on board, including a teacher. And she described
22   their faces to me. The faces of all the pupils. Watching it.
23   Watching it all on the big screen that had been set up in their
24   school ... waiting ... waiting to see history happen.
25   *(Long pause)* The flight lasted nearly eighty seconds before
26   they fell from the sky and plunged into the sea. She read later
27   that some of the crew were still alive after the explosion —
28   still breathing ... still. *(Pause)* But, nobody could survive the
29   impact as it fell into the water. Nobody could survive that.

1   *(Pause)* 'A rocket out of control.' Out of control. *(Pause)*
2   Funny. It had left a mark on my mother. And yet she had
3   never mentioned it. Never said anything about it. *(Pause)*
4   Scott told me once that his parents had visited America
5   at the time of the shuttle launch. They were about five miles
6   away and there were crowds of people watching and it went up
7   and then — and then there was just this mighty sigh of relief.
8   It was the first time, you see. The first time since —   *(Pause)*
9   And here were people who had never met each other before
10   and they were embracing each other and there were tears and —
11   and — and there was just so much relief. Just so much relief ...
12   about strangers. People they would never meet. *(Pause)*
13   I was over at her place for a party ... my mother's house.
14   It was sort of my leaving party. She'd invited lots of family and
15   friends from school — and — and, during the evening, she
16   came up to me — spoke to me — told me the story about ...
17   about the fireworks ... how, after all the excitement, there was
18   nothing left. And — and — and then she whispered in my ear.
19   *(Pause)* 'Don't go up,' she said. 'Don't go ... '
20
21
22
23
24
25
26
27
28
29
30
31
32
33
34
35

Random Women
by Carolyn Carpenter

1   Stephanie   Teen/Young Adult

2

3   *Stephanie, a teenager disturbed by her father's callous behavior,*
4   *is experiencing a personal crisis of frustration and rage. Here, she*
5   *takes her father's mistress, Joy, hostage and confines her in the*
6   *family's attic. With Joy tied up nearby, Stephanie struggles to*
7   *make sense of this dysfunctional family and the grotesque*
8   *recurring dream that haunts her.*

9

10   I used to have this recurring dream where my brothers
11   and I are in this huge shopping mall with my mom. But it's
12   weird because my mom has no legs. So we're pushing her
13   around in one of those old wheelchairs that don't have any
14   arms. And she sits. Precariously balanced. While we resist
15   the urge to dodge around people on one wheel so she'll
16   topple out. And it doesn't matter how many of the five
17   hundred stores we wheel her to. The one she always wants
18   to visit is up four flights of stairs. So we settle for the food
19   court. And then ... every time ... the grand little food court
20   stage lights up. A drum roll echoes from nowhere. The
21   curtain rises. And there he is. In tap shoes. Surrounded by
22   thirty, maybe forty, mannequins. The crowd goes wild.
23   Slowly, he turns. And begins to dismember the
24   mannequins. He passes the limbs to the crowd. Leg. Arm.
25   Head. Torso. The audience takes each grotesque piece.
26   Slides it to their neighbor. He hums. Yanks. Pop! Snap!
27   Crunch! The parts float through the masses. Form a
28   pattern. Each piece, neighbor to neighbor, heading for my
29   mom. We watch as she becomes buried in body parts. And

1 suddenly I can't take it any more. I lay down. Right there.
2 Between the hot dogs and the gyros. Everything stops. He
3 looks at me. Smiles awkwardly. My brothers laugh. Applaud.
4 The polished tile feels so cool against my cheek. Soft
5 somehow. My mom begins to scream. "What are you doing?
6 Are you crazy? Get up. People will notice us! *Notice me!* Get
7 up! Get on the stage and help your father!"
8   And then I wake up. Violent. Angry. Disgusted. Sad ...
9 wanting to come out the other side. *(She looks at Joy and*
10 *shudders.)* I don't spend much of my time in malls these days.
11
12
13
14
15
16
17
18
19
20
21
22
23
24
25
26
27
28
29
30
31
32
33
34
35

Holy Water and Armadillos
by Catherine Segars

1   Lou Godsey   Teen/Young Adult

2

3   *Lou Godsey, a Southern choirgirl with a strict moral code, gives her*
4   *new roommate a glimpse into her wacky childhood. She unearths*
5   *personal memories that are witty and give a good flavor of the local*
6   *color of her "small town" world view. Although her story is a little*
7   *sanctimonious and more than a bit naive, Lou Godsey's innocent*
8   *optimism and impulsive frankness never fail to charm.*

9

10   I was eight years old and Windell Carter dared me to go
11   swimmin' in the church baptismal. That was before I
12   understood that it was holy water. I would never do that
13   now. Windell knew they'd changed choir practice to Tuesday
14   that week and he had poked tiny pinholes in my water wing
15   muscle tubes. I was having myself a good ole time till I
16   started sinkin', which happened to be right when the choir
17   started singin' 'Upon Our Lord's Return, Living Waters Will
18   Flow.' I started flailin' about and water was splashin' all
19   over the choir loft. The ladies started screamin' 'Jesus is
20   comin'! Jesus is comin'!' Aunt Lillian ran right out the front
21   door down Main Street hollerin', 'Hallelujah, our Lord has
22   returned!' Oh, and Aunt Gertrude, God rest her soul,
23   collapsed on the altar ... Oh no! She didn't die on the altar.
24   She died several years later ... when an armadilla' sucked
25   her toes. *(Pause.)*
26   The poor thing was just tryin' to find a warm place to
27   sleep. Andrew, my cousin, didn't shut the door to the
28   basement all the way, and that night the little fella nosed its
29   way into Aunt Gertrude's room and started lickin' her toes

1   which were hangin' off the side of the bed ... No! It didn't
2   scare her to death. Well, I mean, she was scared at first, of
3   course — she screamed to high heaven and woke up the
4   whole house. Aunt Lillian ran to her room just in time to see
5   Aunt Gertrude caress the armadilla's face and cry, 'Oh Walter,
6   oh Walter!' Then she keeled over and died. Walter was her
7   husband who had joined the triumphant choir in the sky thirty
8   years earlier. He apparently had a *(Whisper.)* ... foot fetish.
9   Imagine our surprise.
10   Aunt Gertrude was the founding member of the
11   Cooperstown Temperance Society. Oh, yes. That is a true
12   story. It wasn't exactly dinner conversation, but it spread to
13   every back porch in town. *(Covering her mouth.)* Well, I've been
14   ramblin', haven't I? Granny says that I can talk the ears off a
15   Basset Hound ... Well, I've never actually tried. I think she
16   meant that as a figure of speech.
17
18
19
20
21
22
23
24
25
26
27
28
29
30
31
32
33
34
35

Romeo and Juliet, Part II
by Sandra Hosking

1 Juliet   Young Adult/Adult

2

3 *In this hilarious parody of William Shakespeare's classic*
4 *tragicomedy we get a comic forecast of a young, married, and*
5 *pregnant Juliet! In this scene, Juliet confides in her beloved Nurse —*
6 *whose ashes now reside in an urn! — that she fears growing old and*
7 *that Romeo may no longer love her. There is no elegant blank verse*
8 *here, just a satirical point of view that promises a wealth of lustful*
9 *laughter!*

10

11   Good, they are gone. I pray Friar Lawrence can draw my
12 husband into this present time. Sometimes methinks his
13 mind remains entombed. Aye, me. My back bears the
14 weight of a hundred horses galloping up and down upon it.
15 *(Talking to her stomach.)* I am ready for you. Your bed is made
16 with wool blankets. A dozen sisters await you. How nice a
17 present it would be to have you to wake up to. If you do not,
18 I shall have to cut you out. *(Contraction.)* Oh! *(Relaxes.)*
19   *(She takes a shiny urn off the shelf.)* Oh, Nurse, how I wish
20 you were here in person. *(Looks at her reflection.)* Oh. I am
21 aged. How tired I look. Where is that maiden of yesteryear?
22 She is in the faces of my little ones.
23   Kind, sweet Nurse. My problem now is not my physical
24 state. It is a matter of the heart. It is my Romeo. I fear he
25 no longer loves me. He thinks me fat and old and a crank.
26 Now I know why Mama and Papa maintain separate
27 quarters. And this, dear Nurse, I cannot bear. He speaks in
28 his sleep. I have not told him thus, for things said in sleep
29 are not meant for the light of day, though they eventually

1 have a way of finding illumination. The other night he called
2 out a name ... Rosaline. I cannot discount this utterance. She
3 was his unrequited love. What or why he thinks of her I know
4 not, but my mind is wrought with torturous wondering. I'm
5 afraid my obsession has turned me into a shrew.
6   If you were here, you could tell me not to worry. That I am
7 his only true love. That I am the one he comes home to each
8 day after his meanderings. Here is the rub. I, too, dream of
9 another time. 'Tis hard to remember our humble beginnings.
10 When to be apart was like moving the tide back with a spoon.
11 I cannot help but wonder what life would have been like had I
12 married Paris. Mother reminds me of it each time I see her.
13 Perhaps if I would not have chosen Romeo, I would not have
14 fallen out of my father's favor. And perhaps I would have a big
15 house overlooking Verona such as the thin, fair Rosaline.
16   'Tis no good to think of these things. Thank you, Nurse.
17 Even in death, you comfort me.
18
19
20
21
22
23
24
25
26
27
28
29
30
31
32
33
34
35

For Whom the Southern Belle Tolls
by Christopher Durang

1 Ginny and Lawrence   Teens/Young Adults
2
3   *Duolog*
4   *The duolog, a brief scene for two performers, is an excellent*
5   *opportunity to polish your classroom performance or audition*
6   *skills with a partner. Remember to direct dialog and subtle*
7   *character reactions to your partner in the following scene and*
8   *be aware of potential opportunities to interact with your*
9   *partner whenever possible. Play the scene with an emphasis*
10   *on the special relationship established by the characters and*
11   *use movement, props, and set pieces sparingly as you and*
12   *your partner concentrate on communicating the basic*
13   *ingredients of each character's attitude or mood suggested in*
14   *the given circumstances of the text. Working collaboratively*
15   *with a partner to mutually sketch contrasting character*
16   *portraits will undoubtedly enhance your own individual*
17   *performance skills and spark the intuition and imagination*
18   *needed for a memorable scene.*
19
20   *This biting, wild parody of Tennessee Williams'* **The Glass**
21   **Menagerie** *is alternately funny, outrageous, and shocking in its*
22   *satire. The author's comedy owes much to the Williams' original*
23   *in terms of the characters and the situation, which are well-*
24   *known to theatre veterans — but the comic twists, role reversals,*
25   *and madcap point of view are vintage Durang. The scene in the*
26   *original drama — that is being parodied by Durang — is an*
27   *emotional moment where Tom invites a young man he knows*
28   *to dinner to meet his family. Tom's mother, Amanda,*
29   *immediately seizes this opportunity to promote Laura, her*

45

1   *crippled daughter, as a prime candidate for marriage. Jim, the*
2   *guest caller, is a nice, competitive young man who wins Laura's*
3   *affection and friendship — only to later reveal that he is already*
4   *engaged to be married. In Durang's parody, Tom brings home a*
5   *factory worker (Ginny) as a romantic suitor for his difficult brother*
6   *(Lawrence). In addition to the sex-role reversal, Lawrence is*
7   *portrayed as a "hypochondriac" with psychosomatic ailments and*
8   *a pronounced limp, and Ginny is portrayed as "one of the guys,"*
9   *a hard-working, fast-talking woman who, unfortunately, is also*
10   *hearing impaired!*
11
12   *(Slight silence at the beginning.)*
13 **GINNY:** Hi!
14 **LAWRENCE:** Hi. *(Pause.)* I'd gone to bed.
15 **GINNY:** I never eat bread. It's too fattening. I have to watch
16   my figure if I want to get ahead in the world. Why are you
17   wearing that nightshirt?
18 **LAWRENCE:** I'd gone to bed. I wasn't feeling well. My leg
19   hurts, and I have a headache, and I have palpitations of
20   the heart.
21 **GINNY:** I don't know. Hum a few bars, and I'll see. *(LAWRENCE*
22   *looks at her oddly, decides to ignore her mishearing.)*
23 **LAWRENCE:** We've met before, you know.
24 **GINNY:** *(Not able to hear him.)* Uh huh.
25 **LAWRENCE:** We were in high school together. You were voted
26   Girl Most Likely to Succeed. We sat next to one another
27   in glee club.
28 **GINNY:** I'm sorry, I really can't hear you. You're talking too softly.
29 **LAWRENCE:** *(Louder.)* You used to call me *Blue Roses.*
30 **GINNY:** Blue roses? Oh yes, I remember, sort of. Why did I
31   do that?
32 **LAWRENCE:** I had been absent from school for several
33   months, and when I came back, you asked me where I'd
34   been, and I said I'd been sick with viral pneumonia, but
35   you thought I said 'blue roses.'

1 GINNY: I didn't get much of that, but I remember you now.
2   You used to make a spectacle of yourself every day in
3   glee club, clumping up the aisle with this great noisy leg
4   brace on your leg. God, you made a racket.
5 LAWRENCE: I was always so afraid people were looking at
6   me, and pointing. But then eventually Mama wouldn't let
7   me wear the leg brace anymore. She gave it to the
8   Salvation Army.
9 GINNY: I've never been in the army. How long were you in for?
10 LAWRENCE: I've never been in the army. I have asthma.
11 GINNY: You do? May I see?
12 LAWRENCE: *(Confused.)* See it?
13 GINNY: Well, sure, unless you don't want to.
14 LAWRENCE: Maybe you want to see my collection of glass
15   cocktail stirrers. *(He limps to the table that contains his*
16   *cherished collection of glass cocktail stirrers. GINNY follows*
17   *him amiably, but has no idea what he's talking about.)* I call
18   this one Stringbean, because it's long and thin.
19 GINNY: Thank you. *(Puts it in her glass and stirs it.)*
20 LAWRENCE: *(Fairly appalled.)* They're not for use. *(Takes it*
21   *back from her.)* They're a collection.
22 GINNY: Well I guess I stirred it enough.
23 LAWRENCE: They're my favorite thing in the world. *(Holds up*
24   *another one.)* I call this one Q-tip, because I realized it
25   looks like a Q-tip, except it's made out of glass and
26   doesn't have little cotton swabs at the end of it. *(GINNY*
27   *looks blank.)* Q-Tip.
28 GINNY: Really? *(Takes it and puts it in her ear.)*
29 LAWRENCE: No! Don't put it in your ear. *(Takes it back.)* Now
30   it's disgusting.
31 GINNY: Well, I didn't think it was a Q-tip, but that's what you
32   said it was.
33 LAWRENCE: I call it that. I think I'm going to throw it out
34   now. *(Holds up another one.)* I call this one Pinocchio
35   because if you hold it perpendicular to your nose it

1   makes your nose look long. *(Holds it to his nose.)*

2 GINNY: Uh huh.

3 LAWRENCE: And I call this one Henry Kissinger, because he

4   wears glasses and it's made of glass.

5 GINNY: Uh huh. *(Takes it and stirs her drink again.)*

6 LAWRENCE: They're just for looking, not for stirring. *(Calls*

7   *Off-stage.)* She's making a mess with my collection.

8 GINNY: You know what I take your trouble to be, Lawrence?

9 LAWRENCE: Mama says I'm retarded.

10 GINNY: I know you're tired. I figured that's why you put on

11   the nightshirt, but this won't take long. I judge you to be

12   lacking in self-confidence. Am I right?

13 LAWRENCE: Well, I am afraid of people and things, and I have

14   a lot of ailments.

15 GINNY: But that makes you special, Lawrence.

16 LAWRENCE: What does?

17 GINNY: I don't know. Whatever you said. And that's why you

18   should present yourself with more confidence. Throw

19   back your shoulders and say, *Hi! How ya doin'?* Now you

20   try it.

21 LAWRENCE: *(Unenthusiastically, softly.)* Hi. How ya doin'?

22 GINNY: *(Looking at watch, in response to his supposed question.)*

23   I don't know, it's about 8:30, but this won't take long and

24   then you can go to bed. All right, now try it. *(Booming.)*

25   *Hi! How ya doin'?*

26 LAWRENCE: Hi. How ya doin'?

27 GINNY: Now swagger a bit. *(Kinda butch.) Hi! How ya doin'?*

28 LAWRENCE: *(Imitates her fairly successfully.) Hi! How ya doin'?*

29 GINNY: Good, Lawrence. That's much better. Again. *Hi! How*

30   *ya doin'?*

31 LAWRENCE: *Hi! How ya doin'?*

32 GINNY: *The Braves played a helluva game, don'tcha think?*

33 LAWRENCE: *The Braves played a helluva game, don'tcha think?*

34 GINNY: Hi, Mrs. Wingvalley! Your son Lawrence and I are

35   getting on just fine, aren't we Lawrence?

Chapter III
Coming of Age

The human heart has hidden treasures,
In secret kept, in silence sealed —
The thoughts, the hopes, the dreams,
  the pleasures,
Whose charms were broken —
  if revealed.

— *Charlotte Brontë,* Evening Solace

There is a uniform truth expressed by the monolog characters in this chapter. They are innocent victims with no convenient means of escape from their tormentors. The price they have paid for coming of age cannot be measured in simple words or phrases. Their experiences have taught them that human nature can be cruel and callous, and there are precious few moments of quiet escape from the bitter reality of their lives. Although there is a certain grace and beauty in each character, most have been robbed of sweet childhood memories and are left with searing adolescent scars or shattered adult dreams.

The common denominator that brings each of these monologs into sharp focus is the collective memory of a traumatic event or happening that signals a premature and painful coming of age. The lessons learned here arouse our deeper emotions so that we may examine our own lives with more honesty. The comic or tragic experiences these characters face are commonplace in human nature and should be easy to recognize. But you should also understand that the characters exhibit in their heroic courage, strength, or will to survive an ability to overcome adversity and achieve a measure of personal dignity.

In playing the monologs please note there are limited italicized stage directions or parenthetical clues that may help reveal the "inner truth" of the characters' lives. Be restrained as you explore a more personal tone in voicing the dialog or suggesting character actions or reactions that might give added dimension to the individual portraits. These monolgs also lend themselves to experiments with the alternative performance techniques discussed in chapter I. Allow sufficient time in your rehearsal period to explore the "objective memory" and the "substitution," or transfer, techniques to help flesh out your character portraits in terms of possible mannerisms, personal traits, or posture.

Our Little Secret
by Sandra Fenichel Asher

1   Sue   Teen/Young Adult

2

3   *Sue, a solemn and withdrawn teenager who seems older and*
4   *more world-weary than her years, sits holding a large stuffed*
5   *dog. There is an air of unhappiness that seems to surround her,*
6   *a "fallen victim" look of despair and unhappiness. Sue now*
7   *recalls a painful incident early in childhood and slowly comes to*
8   *terms with her sense of disillusionment and lost innocence.*

9

10   It's been three days since Uncle Jeff died. Wrapped that
11 old Mustang of his around a telephone pole. Funeral was
12 today, and I still can't figure out how I feel. Unless numb is
13 a feeling. Mama's pretty broken up, but he was her baby
14 brother, after all. Daddy said it's just lucky the drunken fool
15 didn't take anybody else with him. That made Mama cry
16 even more. Uncle Jeff moved in with us just before my
17 twelfth birthday. That was six years ago, so I guess he was
18 twenty-seven then. Daddy didn't want him, but Grandpa
19 said we had to take him because it was maybe his last
20 chance — he was in so much trouble already, because of
21 the drinking — and maybe Mama and Daddy could set a
22 good example for him: nice, stable family, hard-working,
23 God-fearing, and clean. Mama, she begged and pleaded with
24 Daddy to do what Grandpa said. So Uncle Jeff moved in. *(A*
25 *beat, a sigh, before continuing.)*
26   And on the night of my twelfth birthday — it was a
27 Sunday, I remember, we'd all been to church — he came
28 into my room real late, after everybody's gone to sleep, and
29 he woke me up with a hand over my mouth. Then he lay

1 down next to me. Seems like I can still smell the beer and
2 cigarettes on him. He started pawing at me then and telling
3 me how pretty I was and how I was a big girl now and he had
4 a nice present for me, but it had to be our little secret, okay?
5 I was never to tell anyone, because if I did, he'd deny he ever
6 touched me and no one would ever believe me. They'd all get
7 mad at me, too, for saying such things. So I was to be a good
8 girl and just take it easy and he promised it would feel nice
9 and I would like it.
10   Only it didn't feel nice. It hurt and I cried. Then he held
11 me — too tight — and told me everything would be just fine,
12 it really would, but he had to do this thing, you see? I was just
13 so pretty, he couldn't stop thinking about me. He couldn't
14 help himself. So if I didn't let him, he'd have to do it with my
15 sister — and Becky, she was only nine years old. I was the big
16 girl, see? So I let him, because I was afraid. And then I went
17 on letting him because I was ashamed. But mostly, I let him
18 for Becky's sake, because my baby sister is the sweetest child
19 in the world and I'd do anything for her. I really would.
20   Only ... this morning, before the funeral, she crept into bed
21 with me, brought this big old stuffed dog with her, like she
22 used to, back when we were just kids, and she said, 'Sue, I
23 have to tell you something, and you have to promise not to get
24 mad at me, okay?' 'Okay,' I said. 'I promise.' And she said,
25 'Sue, Uncle Jeff and I, we had this secret ... '
26
27
28
29
30
31
32
33
34
35

Life Without Parole
by Warren John Doody

1   Grace Klondike   Adult
2
3   *Grace Klondike, a convict serving life in prison for the shooting*
4   *death of her husband, recounts the events that led to the crime:*
5   *her upbringing with an abusive father, the early stages of her*
6   *relationship with an abusive husband, and the night she shot*
7   *him while he slept in bed. This cold and dark true-life story was*
8   *inspired by Elizabeth Dermody Leonard's book* Convicted
9   Survivors: The Imprisonment of Battered Women Who Kill.
10
11   I'm Grace Klondike, and I'm doing life in prison for the
12 shooting death of my husband. There was a lot of violence
13 in my home growing up. My father drank a lot. And when he
14 got drunk, he'd turn on my mother. Just beat the crap out
15 of her for no reason. And then one night, I remember her
16 running into my room and waking us up, and we left the
17 house. We were running away on foot, because she didn't
18 have a car, and when I got too tired to keep up, she held my
19 brother in her arms and put me on her back to carry me, to
20 run, to go. But we didn't get very far. We lasted about a day
21 or two ... there was nowhere to go ... except back home.
22   When I got older, and I knew my mom was going to die,
23 Richard suddenly appeared in my life like a guardian angel.
24 He was everything ... at first. Everything you could imagine.
25 There were some rough edges, but I thought of him like
26 you'd think of a fixer-upper house. He just needed a little
27 bit of this and a little bit of that and it would all be fine. I
28 didn't know any better. I didn't know about the red flags
29 and warning signs of domestic violence.

1   The first time it dawned on me that something might be
2   off was a few months into the relationship. We had been
3   somewhere together, and were returning in separate vehicles,
4   and I had to stop at the supermarket. As I pulled into the
5   parking lot, I saw his car. It was a very unique car, hard to
6   miss. When I got home, I asked him if it was him, and he said,
7   'Yeah.' And I said, 'Well, what were you doing there?' He said,
8   'I was just checking. I wanted to make sure that you were
9   really where you said you were going to be.'
10   Then the criticism started. Just a few things at first. He'd
11 point out something about my cooking, or the way I kept
12 house, or a dress I was wearing, or my hair style. And then we
13 stopped going out, unless it was with his friends. Then he
14 didn't want me to go anywhere unless it was with his friends'
15 wives, or his mother, or with him. He totally controlled me. I
16 was only allowed to walk to the supermarket with my children,
17 and I was only allowed to be gone a certain length of time. If
18 I was gone too long, he would beat me. It got to the point
19 where the kids were begging me, 'Mom, please let's hurry. We
20 don't want Daddy to hurt you when you get home.'
21   He would hit me, and then apologize, and the next
22 paycheck he'd come home with flowers and a card. He was so
23 handsome. And I was not going to give up on this man. I
24 thought, 'If I had cleaned better, if I had picked up the kids'
25 toys better, if I had washed the windows, he wouldn't have
26 thrown the knife through the refrigerator and we wouldn't've
27 had to buy a new one. It's all my fault.'
28   I was at a party when it happened. I was standing outside,
29 next to a car with some friends. He walked by at the exact
30 moment that I laughed at a joke. He thought I was laughing
31 at him, so he took a step forward and backhanded me across
32 the face. And nobody did anything. He pulled my arm behind
33 my back and led me toward the house. And nobody said
34 anything. Then he took me into the bathroom and said, 'No
35 wife of mine is going to laugh at me and get away with it.'

1   Then he started kicking me in the stomach. I curled up in
2   the fetal position, trying not to resist too much, because it would
3   only make things worse. He dragged me into the back bedroom
4   and started hitting me again, swinging at my sides and at my
5   head. He said, 'You aren't going to live to see the morning.'
6   Something inside of me died. He passed out on the bed beside
7   me. I lay there for a while, and my face was hurting ... so I got
8   up and went to the kitchen and got some ice from the
9   refrigerator. There was a gun on top of it. I grabbed the ice and
10 the gun, and walked back into the bedroom.

11   I stood there. I pointed the gun at him, closed my eyes,
12 and pulled the trigger. Someone called the police. I confessed.
13 As part of the case against me, they included something
14 called 'special circumstances.' I asked them, 'What are
15 special circumstances?' They said, 'The death penalty.' The
16 trial lasted three days. Picking a jury lasted two. The drugs
17 they gave me shut me down. I don't remember coming to
18 prison. I don't remember being sentenced. I don't remember
19 going to court. I was so knocked out and in shock that I could
20 not tell you what happened. I don't know if I even testified.

21   One day I went in to talk to a counselor, and she asked
22 me how much time I was serving. The judge told me that even
23 though I had been given a sentence of fifteen to life, that with
24 good behavior I would only be doing seven years, so that's
25 what I told her. She looked at me and said, 'You ain't never
26 getting out of here.' I tried to argue with her, tried to tell her
27 what the judge said, and she told me, 'Honey, the only way
28 you're going to leave this place is in a pine box.'

29   What you're going to find out in a lot of the old-time lifers,
30 like me, is that the Parole Board will make certain
31 recommendations. Things you should do before the next
32 hearing. You do them and the board says, 'Well now, you need
33 to do this,' and then you go out and do those things. And it
34 just keeps going on and on. Eventually, you hit a peak and
35 there's nothing else to do, and that's when you start to

1 regress. You know that no matter what you do, it won't make
2 any difference.
3   I'll probably die in here, with some kind of sickness or
4 something. I've come to that conclusion, and I've accepted it.
5 I just hope that when it does happen, it happens quickly. I've
6 told certain girls in here, friends of mine, that if they notice
7 I'm getting weak and that I'm about to pass on, to come to
8 my cell and take my possessions for themselves. I don't want
9 to leave anything behind. I don't want to be really sick in here,
10 trying to hold on. I just want to die as quickly and peacefully
11 as I can.
12
13
14
15
16
17
18
19
20
21
22
23
24
25
26
27
28
29
30
31
32
33
34
35

Autumn's Child
by Tom Smith

1 Chloe   Young Adult
2
3 *Chloe, a young unmarried woman in her early twenties, returns*
4 *home after the tragic still-birthing of her baby in the hospital.*
5 *Chloe is distracted in her grief, so the actual events or villainous*
6 *schemes she relates to her mother in the following excerpts*
7 *remain a mystery. In the first excerpt, Chloe offers a stark retelling*
8 *of the baby's tragic still-birth death. In the second excerpt, Chloe*
9 *recalls her own heroic efforts to restore the baby to life.*
10
11   It was very quiet, after the final push. No one said a
12 word. Then, suddenly, the doctor begins working real fast,
13 flipping the baby over like it was a rag doll. It's so quiet. The
14 doctor's pulling and turning and ... Finally I say, 'What is it?
15 What's happening?' And a nurse comes over and sponges
16 my forehead. Why is it so quiet? Finally, the doctor looks at
17 me and says, 'I'm sorry. There was no way for us to know.'
18 And he cuts the umbilical cord and walks away. I look up
19 and see the nurse crying. I begin to cry. I'm not sure why. I
20 see another nurse hold up my baby and she dries off the
21 blood with a towel. Why am I crying but my baby is not?
22 Why isn't my baby crying? *(Beat.)*
23   It never occurred to me that she was dead. They're all
24 standing there, thinking she's dead. The doctor comes back
25 over to me and tells me the umbilical cord was wrapped too
26 tight around her neck for too long. The blood couldn't reach
27 the brain. She had strangled herself inside of me ... and she
28 was dead. Then he tells me not to think about it now, but
29 later if I wanted to they would send someone to my room to

1 talk to me. He apologized and left the room. I tried to sit up
2 to look at my baby but the nurse held me down and said I
3 needed to wait for the afterbirth. *(Beat.)*
4   I saw them take her. My baby. They cleaned her up and
5 then put her in a white cloth and then put her and the cloth
6 in a metal tub. I cried out, 'Don't you throw away my baby!
7 Don't you dare throw away my baby. She's not dead! She just
8 needs love. Let me hold my baby and everything will be
9 alright!' Then I felt a needle go into my arm and when I woke
10 up, it was two hours later and they had thrown my baby away.
11 Like she was an old Kleenex. When the psychologist came to
12 see me I didn't say a word. I kept silent, like in the hospital
13 room after the final push. *(Beat.)*
14   They threw my baby away! They didn't know she wasn't
15 dead. They didn't know.
16   • • • • •
17   They were horrible at the hospital, Momma! Horrible! They
18 tried to throw my baby away. I only thank God I was able to
19 find her again. She was in a drawer. In the morgue. The
20 morgue, Momma! I opened the drawer and there she was.
21 Marked 'Dead at Birth.' Shhh, listen to me, Momma. Listen to
22 the miracle.
23   I took the baby from the drawer, and I held her up close
24 against my heart. I knew she was breathing but they just
25 couldn't tell. She was breathing too delicately. I held her
26 close. I kissed her forehead. Did you notice her hair? It's
27 blonde. White blonde. Angel hair. I kiss her forehead. I kiss
28 her on top of her head. And I apologize for everything she's
29 gone through. Then I breathe real deep, to show her how to
30 breathe like us. Less delicately. But she still breathes lightly.
31 So lightly.
32   There's a little tag on her wrist with 'Baby Girl Doe' on it.
33 Momma, how can you be loved without a name? I took the tag
34 off her wrist, and I look down and, still cradling her, I say, 'I
35 name you Angela.' It means angel. Suddenly, she moves a bit.

1 'Angela,' I say real soft, 'It's your momma. You can breathe
2 now. No one will ever take you away from me again. You can
3 live because I love you!' And then — oh, Momma! — Angela
4 started to cry. It was music. Beautiful music! She cried for the
5 first time! It was like I tried to tell the doctors: life can't
6 happen until there's love. She hadn't known any love yet. She
7 cried so loud and so strong that I had to take her out of the
8 hospital. If they had heard her they would have taken her away
9 from me again.
10   They just don't want to believe what love can do. It gave
11 life to Angela. Love is better than anything doctors can do and
12 that's why she's alive now. I proved it to them! Love is better
13 than medicine. Love gives life! And I gave love to Angela.
14
15
16
17
18
19
20
21
22
23
24
25
26
27
28
29
30
31
32
33
34
35

Card Impotence
by Peggy Dunne

1   Dora   Adult
2
3   *Dora, a mature woman who comes from a conservative, suburban*
4   *family with hidden secrets of abuse that mask the family facade*
5   *of perfection, is visited by her older sister, Caitlin. Dora, the lonely*
6   *outsider, is the only one willing to confront the dysfunctional*
7   *clan. She gets her opportunity when the afternoon mail brings*
8   *another in a long line of greeting cards sent by Caitlin.*
9
10 Yes, I'm the irresponsible one. I don't send birthday
11 cards, or Easter cards, or Mother's or Father's Day cards or
12 Christmas cards or Valentines, or Halloween or St. Patrick's
13 Day cards. You could create a full-time job just sending
14 cards three hundred and sixty-five days a year. I actually
15 hate it when I get all the appropriate cards on all the
16 appropriate dates, because all it makes me feel is how
17 efficient you are and how when you don't get one, how
18 disappointed and angry you get at me. And every time I get
19 another pastel pink or violet or baby blue or red or green or
20 orange envelope in the mail — you never send white
21 envelopes — with some *love* stamp on it, I swear I'll be good
22 this year and keep track of everyone's birthdays and all the
23 holidays and send everyone a card and another year passes
24 and I don't.
25 It doesn't make me a bad person. If you're so
26 disapproving then cut me out of your life. Then I wouldn't
27 have to deal with the bull ... of being reprimanded for every
28 'disappointment.' Not with words, mind you. It's always a
29 look or a coolness in your voice — every 'disappointment' I

1 cause you! Maybe I hate that about you! Did you ever think of
2 that? I mean, for God's sake! Did you ever, for a moment,
3 think about that? When were our lives reduced to sending
4 greeting cards? It doesn't mean I don't love you and don't
5 think about you almost every day and tell everyone I know
6 what a wonderful, caring person you are. That you're the one
7 who is full of light and I'm the dark, brooding, negative one.
8 Just stop expecting it from me. It's not who I am. It's never
9 going to happen.
10 Stop waiting for all the cards and you won't be
11 disappointed. I mean you always send me the same card
12 anyway. It's always sparkly and has flowers and some
13 sentimental expression of how I'm the best sister a sister
14 could ever have. Maybe we should just mail the same card
15 back and forth to each other. I don't even read them anymore.
16 I open the envelope, look at the card and throw it away.
17 *(Pause.)*
18 Actually, I love getting cards on my birthday. If I didn't, I
19 probably would feel lonely and that nobody cared about me ...
20 I'm sorry. I'm an awful person. I'm thoughtless and lazy and ...
21 *(Sighs.)* I'm sorry. *(Pause.)* I think maybe it has to do with when
22 I bought you a Mother's Day card when we were kids that said,
23 'Happy Mother's Day, Sis.' I proudly showed it to Mom before
24 I gave it to you and she screamed at me and told me to return
25 it to the store and get my money back. It cost twenty-five
26 cents. I was scared the lady wouldn't take it back, so I tore a
27 little hole in the back of the card and showed the lady and
28 asked her if I could have a refund. She just gave me another
29 card. I was terrified that Mom would ask me about it, so I hid
30 under the bed for three days. Do you think my card impotency
31 has something to do with that?
32
33
34
35

I Knew This One Child
by Rebecca Royce

1 Street Person   Adult
2
3 *A scruffy street person bends over a garbage barrel in a deserted*
4 *alley, pulls out a half-eaten sandwich, brushes it off, and sniffs it.*
5 *She is a disillusioned woman suffering the pangs of despair and*
6 *isolation. Recalling a brutal, shattering event in the life of a child*
7 *she once knew, the street person tries to make sense of the*
8 *nonsense of brutality and violence.*
9
10   **Whewee! I don't think that was any good even before it**
11 **went bad, if ya' know what I mean.** *(Throws the sandwich*
12 *back into the barrel.)* **Why'd somebody wanna eat somethin'**
13 **like that? Liverwurst. What kinda animal does that come**
14 **from, anyway? I just had an avocado and turkey sandwich,**
15 **from down by the other place, back down over there. You**
16 **know that place. The one where all the teenagers hang out.**
17 **Not from the trash, either. This sweet young girl, 'bout**
18 **fifteen or sixteen, she gave me half of her sandwich when**
19 **she saw me goin' through the trash. Gave me a big ole'**
20 **pickle, too, and the rest of her Coca-Cola. There's some**
21 **good people in this world. Some good children. I ain't got**
22 **nothin' against children, even if they get into trouble, 'cause**
23 **they're just learnin'. It's when people grow up, when they're**
24 **adults, that they ain't got no excuse. Like me. I ain't got no**
25 **excuse.**
26   **I knew this one child. She came home one day and her**
27 **daddy had shot her momma. And there was the child, just**
28 **gettin' home from school. She walks in the door and there's**
29 **her momma laying there. And there's blood all around her**

1 head, and her daddy's standin' there with a gun in his hand.
2 That child didn't know what to do, she was so scared. Then,
3 her daddy points the gun at her and pulls the trigger. But that
4 child was fast, and she jumped outta the way and ran over to
5 the neighbor's screamin', 'My momma's dead! My momma's
6 dead!' Well the neighbors, they heard the gunshots and locked
7 up tight, 'cause in that buildin' that's what you did, 'cause you
8 didn't want to be takin' the chance that maybe the next shot
9 was comin' your way. So there was that child, out there
10 bangin' on the neighbor's doors, screamin' and cryin', and
11 nobody would let her in.
12 But I guess somebody called the police, 'cause just as her
13 father came out into the hallway and raised his gun, a police
14 officer came up the stairs and shot him dead. She didn't even
15 say, 'Drop the gun, or I'll shoot!' She couldn't take the chance
16 that he would shoot the child. That police officer was young
17 herself. Just out of the academy. The end of her second week
18 on the job. *(Reaches inside her coat and takes out a bottle. Twists*
19 *off the cap and drinks.)*
20 I know what you're thinkin'. You're thinkin' that man was
21 just trash. Some drunk, or some crazy animal to be killin' his
22 wife and tryin' to kill his own child. But that ain't how that
23 child saw it. She ran over to her daddy, cryin' and tryin' to
24 help him up. She kept sayin', over and over, 'I'm sorry, Daddy.
25 I'm sorry, Daddy.' That's how kids see things. Like it was their
26 fault. There's almost no tellin' 'em different. 'Cause they think
27 the whole world revolves around them, 'til they learn that it
28 don't. *(Takes another drink.)*
29 I don't know what happened to that child. That officer
30 went to the hospital, to get her nose looked at, I suppose. But
31 I don't know what happened to her, either. *(Looks back in the*
32 *trash barrel. Digs around a little.)* I ain't hungry. I just had a nice
33 sandwich, and a pickle. That pickle was good, I'm gonna go
34 back there, see if I can't get me another one. *(Exits.)*
35

The Battered Wife
by Ernest Slyman

1 Wife	Young Adult/Adult

2

3 *This narrative poem highlights fundamental character traits*
4 *related to battered women throughout recorded history. It is a*
5 *universal story that voices the fear, frustration, and personal crises*
6 *suffered by innocent victims of domestic abuse and violence. It*
7 *also offers an intimate glimpse of a woman's world in which*
8 *unprovoked acts of hostility and violence are common.*

9

10   The first time
11   you crushed my skull
12   I was happy,
13   but that was a thousand years ago.

14

15   I have been tossed from windows
16   and set aflame as I slept in bed.
17   I have been shot in the head,
18   gagged and dropped from a train.
19   I have been poisoned
20   and left in the dark beside a road.
21   I have given birth to a thousand children,
22   and each one I loved.

23

24   You were tall in France,
25   and short in Spain,
26   and often handsome
27   and occasionally bald and fat —
28   with blue eyes in Austria
29   and brown eyes in Italy.

1   You drank vodka from a hat
2   and played the violin.
3
4   You were Jack in England,
5   Juan in Peru,
6   and Tom in Hungary.
7   (What was that tune
8   you were always whistling?)
9
10   During the Ch'in dynasty
11   you bloodied my face
12   and broke my arm.
13
14   You cursed at me
15   every day for centuries.
16   I have wept in many centuries.
17   You have scorned me too long.
18
19   Never have I hidden from you.
20   Always I met you at the station,
21   greeted you with a kiss.
22
23   You placed flowers on my grave —
24   not once have you wept.
25   I lay still in my favorite dress.
26
27   You cursed at me
28   every day for centuries.
29   I have died in many centuries.
30   I shall come again
31   and wait for you at the station.
32
33
34
35

Memories of Viola
by Jim Danek

1 Viola   Adult

2

3   *Viola Warner, a reclusive widow in a small town in northern*
4   *Wisconsin, recounts the story of her father's death in response to*
5   *a neighbor's question regarding the fact that she never drinks and*
6   *that her father used to be the town sheriff. There is some small*
7   *town social satire here, but for the most part Viola's tale*
8   *glamorizes the life of her cunning father with mirth and laughter.*

9

10   You never heard the story of my father's death?

11   My parents got into it one night during a particularly bad
12 winter. Father stormed out of the house around midnight with
13 his shotgun in one hand and a huge bottle of Jack Daniels in
14 the other. Have no idea what he was expecting to shoot in the
15 dark in the middle of winter. Two days later Deputy Hendricks
16 found the shotgun at the foot of Twin Bridge.

17   He was convinced papa was on the ice and got too close
18 to the flowage. Sure enough, they found him the next spring
19 down there by the dam. Dredged him up from the bottom of
20 the lake, bottle of Jack Daniels still clutched in his hand.
21 Petrified was more like it. After cussing him out good
22 enough, mama insisted that he be buried just the way they
23 found him. She had Mr. Nye, the funeral director, lay that
24 shotgun along side his right side, and with his left arm
25 sticking up out of that coffin clutching that bottle of Jack,
26 papa was sure one sorry sight to behold.

27   Don't think that didn't scare the bejesus out of an entire
28 generation of youth. Every mother from here to Green Bay
29 dragged their kids to that wake. The funeral home suddenly

1   became a three-ring circus with all those mothers dragging their
2   kids in to see papa and yelling, 'See! See! That's what's going
3   to happen to you if you ever let alcohol pass your lips.' I got the
4   impression the kids thought it was all kind of funny. The dead
5   sheriff with one arm sticking up out of his coffin. For the next
6   two years the sale of Jack Daniels increased down at the local
7   watering hole ... in honor of papa ... or so I'm told. *(Pause.)*
8   Heck of a way to see your father leave this earth.
9   *(Laughing.)* But it was either that or mama was going to put
10 him in the coffin box face down. Said it would make it easier
11 for him to dig his way to hell!
12
13
14
15
16
17
18
19
20
21
22
23
24
25
26
27
28
29
30
31
32
33
34
35

The Princess of Rome, Ohio
by Jonathan Joy

1   Lulu   Young Adult/Adult
2
3   *Lulu, an escaped convict accused of manslaughter, explains to*
4   *her friend Alma the events that led to her escape from a Logan*
5   *County, West Virginia prison and later arrival in Rome, Ohio. Lulu*
6   *is cunning and fearless, with a devilish and unbridled spirit.*
7   *There is no indication that she has resolved the emotional*
8   *intensity or internal conflict of her crime.*
9
10   I never told you a lot of things. Now listen close. This is
11 just between the two of us. Nobody else needs to know
12 about it. Nobody. This is my life we're talking about. Not
13 even Bertie Lou. 'Cause you tell her and the whole town'll
14 know before the sun goes down. *(Pause.)* Me leaving Bud
15 didn't exactly happen the way I told you before. I kind of
16 killed him. On accident. It wasn't planned ahead of time or
17 anything. I think they call it manslaughter on the *Law and*
18 *Order* show. I was trying to teach him a lesson. You see, he
19 was going out on me, doing me just like Chester's been
20 doing to you. He was working a lot of late nights, which I
21 knew was a pack of lies 'cause he'd always come home on
22 these nights smelling like whiskey and cheap perfume and
23 then he'd pass out on the couch. This was happening three
24 or four nights a week, and I just couldn't take it anymore.
25   So this night I made the couch real nice for him. I put
26 down a sheet and everything so he'd be nice and
27 comfortable. He comes home as usual and in a few seconds
28 he's out cold. I got my sewing kit out and I took that sheet
29 he was laying on and wrapped him up in it and tied him real

1 tight inside. It took almost an hour to sew him up in it. He
2 never budged once. I was sewing the whole time scared to
3 death he might wake up and find out what I was doing. I got
4 him all tied up in that sheet like he was in a cocoon or
5 something. Then I grabbed the broom out of the kitchen
6 closet and came back and with the wooden handle end I
7 started beating him with it. I just pounded away on him like
8 a Mexican kid with a pinata. It didn't take much of this to
9 wake him up and he started cussing and struggling — only he
10 couldn't do nothing about it 'cause you know ...

11   I really should have stopped there. I know that I should
12 have stopped. To be honest, I was having a lot of fun listening
13 to him squeal and cry like a baby. I was yelling all kinds of
14 stuff to him about chasing skirts and drinking too much and
15 neglecting his wife and little girl at home. I'm figuring the
16 whole time that this is gonna teach him a lesson, right? Right?
17 And it would've, only I got a little carried away and after ten
18 or fifteen minutes of this I noticed that he wasn't struggling
19 anymore. He wasn't sayin' nothing either. And the white sheet
20 that I'd laid out for him wasn't white anymore but it was all
21 covered in red blotchy spots. And the spots were heavier and
22 drippin' in some places, like where his head was. So I knew
23 that at this point maybe I'd gone too far. Maybe that I'd killed
24 him even.

25   Not on purpose, mind you. I blame the whole thing on *The*
26 *Enquirer.* I'd read this story about Willie Nelson and his
27 second wife. Apparently she was having the same kind of
28 problem with him and so she devised this plan, about the
29 same one I used on Bud. It worked for her. Straightened ole
30 Willie right up. I figured if it was good enough for the former
31 Mrs. Willie Nelson then it was good enough for me. I didn't
32 reckon that I'd get as carried away as I did. *(Silence.)*

33   To be honest, I didn't feel that bad about it. Still don't.

34

35

The Colors of Childhood
by Tami Canaday

1   Julia   Young Adult/Adult
2
3   *Julia, now a young adult, is reflecting on her childhood and offers*
4   *a sensitive and expressive account of an unsuspecting incident that*
5   *changed her life when she was just twelve years old. There is the*
6   *anger and disbelief that often accompanies trauma for one so*
7   *young in life, but Julia voices her heartache and sorrow with a*
8   *tenderness that is compassionate and compelling.*
9
10   Afterwards, I remember, when I got back to my
11 neighborhood, I saw my home was no longer red-bricked, no
12 longer white-trimmed, but a cavalcade of maroon, white,
13 silver, yellow, blue, purple, pink, red, white, maroon ...
14 silver ... yellow ... funneling, pouring out like the end of the
15 world ... puddled. But then I was only twelve.
16   Earlier that afternoon, I had snuck out of my
17 neighborhood ... crossed Colfax Avenue over to the west
18 side of Lakewood. It was the bygone time of Lakewood when
19 tin trailers with maroon shutters and white lattice churches
20 sat side-by-side. I believe the air was sunshiny. At least, I
21 want to believe. I am sure, though, I had fervently talked to
22 myself, while I kicked a stone off the sidewalk curves, down
23 the side streets all the way to Kincaid's ... an old pharmacy.
24 I have warm memories of its interior. The rag-wiped silver
25 lunch counter. The Archie comic book display. And right
26 next to the cash register ... the Trojan condom boxes with
27 their yellow-hued photos.
28   Now, the back of Kincaid's, where I always entered, was
29 connected to a laundromat by a narrow three-sided

1 courtyard. A courtyard filled with trash, tossed needles, and
2 ragweed. That day, I saw a man standing in one of its
3 shadowed corners. A man holding a paper sack. He glanced
4 up. Over the years, in my adult disquietude, I've often
5 reflected back to this day and it has always puzzled me why I
6 stopped. The man, too, was skeptical and not quite believing
7 it when I stood still. I remember a light blue crucifix pinned
8 onto his heavy coat, close-cropped hair on a small head, and
9 eyes that cut like diamonds. Oh, maybe, I'm simply shaping
10 ... recreating my memories of him. But I do know he had
11 crosshatches of purple lines on his nose and cheeks. After
12 drinking from his paper sack, he tossed it aside and was
13 quiet. Have you ever taken a step to take a step to take a step
14 and known you were going to fall?
15   Afterwards, when I was stumbling home, all I could think
16 of was did he notice my panties said Saturday, not Sunday
17 like the day it was? Panties, which had hung on one leg like a
18 limp, pink flag until he was through. He had politely helped me
19 to step back fully into my panties, but after that I withstood
20 any further politeness. When I got back to my neighborhood,
21 running down the street, I saw my home was no longer red-
22 bricked, no longer white-trimmed, but a cavalcade of maroon,
23 white, silver, yellow, blue, purple, pink, red, white, maroon ...
24 silver ... yellow funneling, pouring like the blood on my leg.
25 The end of the world ... puddled on the street.
26
27
28
29
30
31
32
33
34
35

Yesterday Came Too Soon
by Jamal Williams

1 Dorothy Dandridge   Adult

2

3 *The life story of legendary African-American blues singer Dorothy*
4 *Dandridge remains a puzzling, unsolved riddle. She was a*
5 *madcap, talented woman relentless in the pursuit of her art and*
6 *career. But there was also a dark side to her life, one that was*
7 *filled with physical abuse, drugs, and depression. Here is an*
8 *intimate glimpse of the "divine" singer as a young woman*
9 *confronting her demons.*

10

11   This marriage started out like the first, badly. We fought
12 on our honeymoon night in San Francisco. He wanted to cut
13 it short so that I could return to Los Angeles to sing at a
14 cabaret gig he'd arranged. We moved into an elegant house
15 in the Hollywood Hills just down the street from Sammy
16 Davis, Jr. and fought like the three dogs we owned. It
17 seemed Jack always needed money ... my money. Money for
18 his manicures, money for his hair stylist, his clothes, his
19 business agent.
20   We owed the cleaners, grocers, gardener, pool man,
21 bank, and my psychiatrist. I was the one bringing home the
22 bacon. The only bacon he was bringing home was the kind
23 you bought from the deli. I lost a lot of money on a
24 restaurant that he opened in Hollywood with me, of course,
25 as the mainliner. I poured my cash down that sinkhole. I
26 had five thousand dollars to my name. The bill collectors
27 were hounding me. Jack, my gentleman husband, allowed
28 me an uncontested divorce. The final resolution was
29 delivered to me just in time for my home to be foreclosed.

1   While the furniture movers were taking my stuff out the door,
2   and the dogs were running around like crazy, I turned and
3   there stood Haroldlynn with two suitcases, abandoned on my
4   front doorsteps because I owed the keeper, too.

5   Drug-like, I moved around the house in the midst of chaos
6   while Haroldlynn, quite unaware of me, played the C-scale on
7   the piano over and over again till I finally said, 'Please stop it,
8   Lynn.' *(Scales get louder.)* It was a melodramatic scene right
9   out of a B-movie. She was unconcerned that we both had
10   nowhere to live. She was a happy twenty-year-old woman with
11   a happy three-year-old mind. God blesses the child that
12   doesn't know. I said again, 'Lynn, baby, please stop!'

13   I should have been crying, but I was too confused to do
14   even that. As the movers went about their job, and my
15   furniture went out the door, I watched as my life went down
16   the whirling cesspool of failure. If there was ever a time that
17   suicide was a consideration, it was then. 'Lynn, please!' *(The*
18   *piano gets louder.)* 'Please, please Lynn, I can't take it. Stop for
19   mommy's sake.' *(She holds her ears.)* '**Lynnnn! Stop!**' *(The*
20   *music stops.)*

21

22

23

24

25

26

27

28

29

30

31

32

33

34

35

Mirrors Remembered
by Cary Wong

1 Montgomery   Young Adult/Adult
2
3 *Montgomery, a young Asian-American artist, is diagnosed with a*
4 *fatal disease. As she reflects on her life of artistic accomplishment*
5 *and promise, images of her mother's death remind her of the*
6 *inevitable reality she also faces. Montgomery doesn't exhibit any*
7 *anger or bitterness as she contemplates the mystery of death, but*
8 *raises serious questions about the meaning of life for an artist.*
9
10   I'm sitting in the hospital waiting room. It's cold. Why is it
11 always so cold in these places? I'm looking at this painting of
12 a sunset. A crude but accurate rendition of one. Glowing red
13 and orange. Reflected on the ocean's surface. I remembered
14 how when I was a little girl, that's all I drew with my Crayola
15 crayons. So simple, so reassuring, so naive. *(Pause.)*
16   The nurse brought me into the room. It was dark except
17 for the fluorescent light above her head. She laid there with
18 her eyes closed, with tubes attached to her arm. I've never
19 seen my mother like that before. I didn't recognize her at
20 first. She had always been so strong. A single mother with
21 a daughter who had crazy notions in her head. That's what
22 she thought of my work. 'Oh, Montgomery, where do all
23 these crazy notions come from?' It didn't mean she didn't
24 like them, she just didn't know how I came to see the world
25 the way I did. She always smiled at my work, not knowing
26 that some of my work wasn't supposed to provoke smiles.
27 She gave me that smile again when she opened her eyes
28 and saw me. I guess my heart was broken after all. *(Pause.)*
29   She was at the supermarket. She said she picked up a

1 quart of milk to look at the expiration date, and the next thing
2 she knew, she was on the floor in this pool of milk. People ran
3 to her, yelling and staring. The worst, she said, was that they
4 didn't think she understood English. They kept yelling, as if
5 that would help her understand. She wanted to yell back, 'I
6 understand English. I can speak English.' Yet, at that
7 moment, she couldn't speak English. Nothing came out of her
8 mouth at all. The rest was a haze of bright lights, spoiled milk,
9 and being jostled around. She said she was so happy when
10 she opened her eyes and saw my familiar face. *(Pause.)*
11 Who was this little woman in this bed? When my father left,
12 it forced my mother to improve her English. But, when I was
13 growing up, I was so embarrassed by her lack of language. I took
14 French in high school, and I quickly realized I would never fully
15 adapt to a second language. And here was my mother, who did
16 it without the help of any textbook. Just old Montgomery Clift
17 movies and the radio. Meanwhile, my Chinese was almost non-
18 existent. I wish I had learned her language as well as she learned
19 mine. She was able to comfort me when I scraped my knee
20 playing street hockey with the boys, when I got my divorce, and
21 when I found out I couldn't have children. 'That's why your art is
22 so important to you,' she would say. 'They're your children.' I
23 thought of this as I hugged my mother in the hospital bed. I
24 knew I couldn't comfort my mother, who, as it would turn out,
25 would be dead by the end of the week. How could I when I knew
26 that soon I would be the one under the fluorescent lights with
27 uncomfortable eyes looking down at me? People who seem to be
28 in more pain than you are. *(Pause.)*
29 As I held my mother that night, hearing her gasping for her
30 next breath, smelling the residue of milk still in her hair, I
31 knew I couldn't lessen her pain. The pain of her loss is still
32 with me. It hasn't diminished one bit. *(Pause.)*
33 Who will be there when I die? My art? Small consolation for
34 a life.
35

I Never Asked
by Elyzabeth Gregory Wilder

1   Woman   Adult

2

3   *A mature white woman retells the story of her infatuation with*
4   *an African-American classmate from childhood. There is a gentle*
5   *sweetness in the childhood memory, but what surfaces most*
6   *vividly is the personal sense of loss and regret that gives the*
7   *monolog its quiet and understated intensity. The woman also*
8   *raises serious questions about traditional values and the*
9   *unyielding social customs of the times.*

10

11   I said I'd have to ask.

12   We were on the playground. At school. You and your
13 sister were wearing your matching dresses with the
14 petticoats that made them stick out like ball gowns. And
15 your patent leather shoes with the fold-down socks with
16 lace trim. You were trying to teach me how to jump rope. I
17 was hopeless. We just kept laughing until we all fell down.
18 Me in my dirty hand-me-downs and you and your sister
19 dressed like you were going to church. Only that's how you
20 dressed every day.

21   I wanted hair like yours. With braids and twists. And the
22 beads that hit against each other in perfect rhythm when
23 you walked. You said my hair was too straight to hold beads
24 so I went home and I put my hair in about a million braids
25 and then I put aluminum foil on the ends to hold the beads
26 in place. But my mother made me take them out.

27   You asked if we could be friends. Remember? And I said
28 I'd have to ask. I don't know why. My mother wouldn't care.
29 She had a lot of friends at work who were black. But they

1 weren't the same kind of friends. They didn't come over for
2 dinner. Or go shopping together. Not really. And at five years
3 old I knew that.
4   And the next day on the playground you wanted to jump
5 rope and I said I was busy playing on the monkey bars.
6 Because I didn't know what else to say. So you and your sister
7 went off and jumped rope and I watched from across the
8 playground as your petticoats bounced and your beads kept
9 the time.
10   And I never asked.
11
12
13
14
15
16
17
18
19
20
21
22
23
24
25
26
27
28
29
30
31
32
33
34
35

The Woman Who Cooked Her Husband
by Debbie Isitt

1 Hilary   Adult
2
3 *Hilary, a mature middle-age woman, has been married to Kenneth*
4 *for a long time. He, however, is now pursuing another woman,*
5 *Laura. In this black comic monolog, Hilary the deserted wife is*
6 *preparing a meal for Laura and Kenneth — a meal neither of them*
7 *is likely to digest or forget! Her menu is a tasty serving of anger,*
8 *betrayal, deceit, frustration, and a generous helping of humiliation.*
9
10   (*She is singing* Stardust Melody. *She notices the audience*
11 *and stops, as if taken by surprise. She stands behind the table.*
12 *To the audience.*)
13   The kitchen is a murderer's paradise. Saucepans crack,
14 knives chop, scissors stab, matches burn, microwaves
15 electrocute, kettles of boiling water scald — the possibilities
16 are endless — especially when you have an axe to grind.
17   It's funny really — considering we spend most of the time
18 in the kitchen — why is it male murderers often want to cook
19 their victims? I'm surprised they know how. But me — I'm an
20 expert cook. I can disguise anything — the times I've served
21 up yesterday's remains and with a little bit of this and a little
22 bit of that — called it by a French name and fooled my
23 husband into thinking he was eating something truly fresh
24 and exotic. Well, food — like sex — is all in the mind.
25   Kenneth went to great lengths to encourage my interest
26 in everything culinary. Well naturally, husbands want their
27 wives to be good and careful cooks — their very health

1 depends on it. But how foolishly they trust, these men — how
2 lacking in suspicion. How many wives have pondered poison
3 while stirring in the gravy, then backing down at the last
4 minute, just spat in it instead — it's food for thought though,
5 isn't it?

6   It has taken me a long time to discover that even though
7 I'm single and have been for many years, I'm still not free. I am
8 suffering from the ex-wife syndrome, a bleak vision of the future
9 has overtaken me — an image of myself growing old, alone,
10 loving no one ever again. I am plagued by fantasies of him
11 making love to her — still, now. I am upset that he looks good,
12 been able to move on with his life, because, when I look at
13 myself in the mirror, I see an image of a woman who doesn't
14 measure up, one who has been banished to the sidelines and
15 replaced. I see nothing more than Kenneth's ex-wife.

16   Since the day he left me, obsessive thoughts have been
17 slipping in and out of my mind, shocking, morbid ideas. That day,
18 I was mincing some meat for my dinner and I had a spark —
19 what would it be like to mince his flesh — would he make a good
20 steak or a better bolognaise — he's such a beefy man — not
21 just skin and bone — he's really meaty — I can just smell the
22 garlic on his breath — it's enough to frighten anyone to death.
23
24
25
26
27
28
29
30
31
32
33
34
35

Romeo and Juliet, Part II
by Sandra Hosking

1   Juliet and Romeo   Young Adults/Adults

2

3   *Duolog*

4   *This inventive parody of William Shakespeare's* **Romeo and**

5   **Juliet** *dutifully attempts to chronicle what the "star-crossed*

6   *lovers" domestic household might have been like had they*

7   *lived and then married. Romeo, the rebellious youth, and*

8   *Juliet, the virtuous maiden, are a sober and much older*

9   *couple in this interpretation of the Shakespeare classic. The*

10   *dialog here is not as lyrical as the blank verse of the original*

11   *text, but there is sparkling word play and comic innuendo*

12   *that gives the characters a more contemporary identity. In*

13   *approaching the scene, try to imagine the psychological*

14   *motivation at work in the word games the characters play*

15   *and try not to appear deliberately cruel or hostile in the verbal*

16   *exchanges that result from anxiety or frustration. Although*

17   *the characters exhibit a serious tone in the scene, peer*

18   *beneath their solemn mood to discover the potential comic*

19   *response that will give a sense of individual, personal identity*

20   *to the more mature Romeo and Juliet.*

21

22   *The bloom is now off the rose, and an older and wiser*

23   *Romeo and Juliet carp and snipe at each other like an old*

24   *married couple. Domestic family life is not as romantic as*

25   *they may have imagined in their youth, and it appears that*

26   *this is as good as it is ever going to get! In this opening*

27   *scene, a very perturbed and pregnant Juliet scolds Romeo*

28   *for being a lazy dreamer.*

29

1 JULIET: *(Calling Off-stage.)* **Romeo! Romeo! Where art thou**
2   **Romeo? Get your arse in here!** *(Sigh.)* **Aye me.**
3 ROMEO: *(Entering.)* **What Juliet?**
4 JULIET: **What? What do you think? Am I not slaving here? Do**
5   **you not see that I am with child? Your child?**
6 ROMEO: **What? No 'good eve' for your true love Romeo.**
7 JULIET: **Ha! Fetch me the plates from the shelf.**
8 ROMEO: **The babes are abed?**
9 JULIET: **Aye they are. Fed, washed, and safely tucked in by**
10   **their mother. Fat cow that she is.** *(He hands her two plates.)*
11   **I need another.**
12 ROMEO: **Who is the third party at my table? I pray 'tis not your**
13   **father.**
14 JULIET: **Why not my father?**
15 ROMEO: **Know you not how he needles me?**
16 JULIET: **I call it guiding.**
17 ROMEO: **Goading. He does not respect my work.**
18 JULIET: **What work is that?**
19 ROMEO: **I am a poet.**
20 JULIET: **A fop. You dream of poetry. The proof is in the sheaf.**
21 ROMEO: *(Sarcastic.)* **You are the flower of cordiality. Prithee put**
22   **my mind at ease, dear wife.**
23 JULIET: **Relax. My father is safe within the walls of his own**
24   **courtyard. Though I should invite him to supper to spite**
25   **you. No, rest easy, Love. It is Friar Lawrence who comes.**
26 ROMEO: **Aah. The good friar. I should lock up the wine then.**
27   **Last time he drank himself into a river.**
28 JULIET: **Where have you been today? Did you speak to the**
29   **silversmith as Papa suggested?**
30 ROMEO: **I did begin my journey there, but was captured by a**
31   **glorious column of trees all aglow with white blossoms.**
32   **Their petals fell to the ground as snow. It reminded me of**
33   **our wedding, Mo Cheri. I settled in to watch the scene for**
34   **but a moment, and my eyes closed as if under a spell.**
35 JULIET: **You tarried.**

1   ROMEO: I was bewitched.

2   JULIET: You slept all day!

3   ROMEO: I was lost.

4   JULIET: You sloth! You snail! Sicilian slug! You are as slow

5   as an old woman walking up a steep hill. All the world

6   moves 'round her while she inches upward. Papa was right

7   about you.

8   ROMEO: Popinjay.

9   JULIET: Clog.

10 ROMEO: Argh. Your voice is as thunder. I am no slug. And

11   your father knows nothing of it.

12 JULIET: No work. No trade. No money. A dozen. A dozen —

13   soon to be 13 — mouths to feed in this hovel. What shall I

14   feed them? Dirt and grubs? Shall I dress the children of

15   Romeo Montague in sackcloths? Where shall we live when

16   you dream your means away? Romeo. Romeo. Your name

17   brings laughter to the people in the town. Do you not hear

18   what they say when we walk Verona's streets? 'Look

19   there,' they say, 'there go poor Romeo's urchins and his

20   vericose wife. Make way for the monkey Montagues!'

21 ROMEO: There was a time when we cared not a whit about the

22   words of others. We ignored their stares and whispers.

23   Remember?

24 JULIET: I can only remember what I see before me. I'll endure

25   it no longer, my husband.

26 ROMEO: What can you do to manage the beasts of the town?

27 JULIET: Money.

28 ROMEO: Money?

29 JULIET: I aim to tame the town with money.

30 ROMEO: Where comes this money?

31 JULIET: I shall work.

32 ROMEO: What?

33 JULIET: Are you deaf?

34 ROMEO: I am dumb. What shall be your trade?

35 JULIET: I shall bake bread and sell it in the square.

1   ROMEO: My wife, a common peddler?
2   JULIET: Better to be industrious than feeble minded. I'll not
3   dwell in the kitchen while my husband wanders as a
4   feckless fly.
5   ROMEO: Feckless?
6   JULIET: I go to fetch water.
7   ROMEO: Let me help.
8   JULIET: No. Rest. It is your best occupation.
9
10
11
12
13
14
15
16
17
18
19
20
21
22
23
24
25
26
27
28
29
30
31
32
33
34
35

Chapter IV

The Age of Rebellion

Build for yourself a strong-box,
Fashion each part with care;
When it's strong as your hand can
Make it,
Put all your troubles there.

— *Bertha Adams Backus,* Then Laugh

In the age of rebellion, monolog characters are often engaged in the struggle for independence and personal values or the conflict between duty to oneself and duty to others. Their struggle for dignity, individuality, and self-identity expresses itself most often in anxiety, fear, frustration, or self-doubt. The behavior of rebellious characters is more directly related to failed personal relationships, social adjustment problems, or the sense of isolation. That behavior is subsequently acted out in aggressive action, verbal abuse, physical conflict, or forceful episodes of intimidation. But there are also comic and farcical acts of rebellion that may resemble fantasy wish-fulfillment, subconscious dreams, silly self-identity crises, or absurd distortions of reality that provoke humor.

These are rather ordinary characters performing non-heroic actions, but there is a frank and genuine treatment of them that underlines their basic individuality. Because these are ordinary characters, the dialog is everyday speech and is sometimes punctuated with slang, colloquialism, or the vernacular to disguise hidden meanings or points of view. The characters may slur syllables, swallow the endings of words, or there may be a series of inarticulate grunts or groans indicated in the script to help communicate a character's attitude. There is, however, a heightened sense of emotional intensity in the rebellious characters that is more closely related to their troubled everyday experiences or observations of daily life.

In playing the monologs it will be important to create the illusion that what is heard or seen is spontaneous, familiar, and natural. Movement, for example, may be less fluid or graceful to capture a character's familiar everyday walk. You should be alert to events in everyday life and to interesting people in all walks of life that may provide the attitude, gesture, mannerism, voice, or walk for rebellious characters. No attempt should be made to actively engage the audience, however, other than to hold their attention as they "eavesdrop" on the dialog. The audience should recognize the resemblance of rebellious characters to real-life role models they may have observed themselves. There is little opportunity in these monologs for elegant posing or pretentious speech.

Junk

by Melvin Burgess
stage adaptation by John Retallack

1 Gemma   Teen
2
3 *In this stage adaptation of the popular Melvin Burgess British*
4 *adolescent novel, fourteen-year-old Gemma runs away from her*
5 *suburban home with her boyfriend, Tar. Eager to escape the rules*
6 *and regulations of their parents and society, the duo is soon*
7 *involved in crime, drugs, and prostitution. Here, the adventurous*
8 *Gemma explains the basic "how to" rules of running away*
9 *successfully.*
10
11   Well, here it is — what you've been waiting for, Gemma
12 Brogan's practical handbook to running away from home. A
13 step-by-step guide:
14   One. You will need: Clothes — woolly vest, plenty of
15 keep-warm stuff. Plenty of underwear and other personal
16 items. A waterproof coat. A personal stereo. A sleeping
17 bag. A pencil and paper. Money. Your father's bank card
18 and PIN number.
19   Two. Your wits. You'll need 'em.
20   Three. Think about it. What are your mum and dad
21 going to do? Try to get you back. Of course. It'll be police.
22 It'll be, oh, my God, my little girl has been abducted. It'll be,
23 maybe some dreadful pervert is at her right now. Maybe
24 she's lying murdered in a bin liner in the town rubbish tip
25 *this very second!* It never occurs to them that little Lucinda
26 got so fed up with Mumsy and Dadsy that she actually left
27 of her own accord. So ... if you don't want every copper in
28 the land on your tail and pictures of you shining out of

1   all the national newspapers, you tell your mum and dad
2   exactly what you're doing.
3   Four. This is where the pencil and paper comes in. You
4   write them a note explaining that you're going away. Wish
5   them luck, tell them no hard feelings and that you hope they
6   will understand.
7   Five. Book your coach ticket using your father's Visa card.
8   Six. Go to the cash machine — take the money — and run.
9   Thank you, very much.
10
11
12
13
14
15
16
17
18
19
20
21
22
23
24
25
26
27
28
29
30
31
32
33
34
35

Dress Up
by Erin Murtaugh

1   Emily   Young Adult/Adult

2

3   *Emily, a spirited but slightly intoxicated young woman wearing*
4   *a pink feather boa, reveals her disappointment about the night to*
5   *a fellow club-goer. Sitting at a bar in a noisy nightclub with a*
6   *drink in front of her, she offers a sensitive look at what it means*
7   *to be a swinging single in the late-night urban jungle. Emily may*
8   *feel inadequate in this setting, but she has the strength and will*
9   *to recognize her mistakes.*

10

11   I hurt my ankle on the dance floor ... just giving it a
12   rest. *(Pause. She looks down at herself.)* **You know the pink**
13   **boa is just a joke. I don't normally dress like this. I don't**
14   **wear fishnet stockings and black vinyl dresses. I guess this**
15   **is vinyl, or is it latex? No, that's what they make condoms**
16   **out of. Anyway, this isn't my usual attire. It was my friend's**
17   **idea, Jessie.** *(She looks around.)*
18   **She's over there ... somewhere. She wanted us to wear**
19   **wigs too, but that's where I drew the line. Actually we just**
20   **couldn't find wigs. The plan was to not be ourselves tonight.**
21   **We were going to dress up really crazy and just be**
22   **somebody else. Somebody glamorous and free-spirited.**
23   **We're both computer technicians. Jessie said that when**
24   **we put on these shiny vinyl dresses then we'd feel really**
25   **sexy. Like we were dominatrixes ... or something. But when**
26   **I put it on I didn't feel sexy, I actually just felt kind of fat.**
27   **See how it bunches up around here? So I thought that**
28   **maybe it would be the atmosphere of the club that would**
29   **transform me. You know, the music and the lights ... the**

1   crowd. But when I got there I just felt worse.
2   I could see the transformation in Jessie though. As soon
3   as she walked in here she was following the plan. She was ...
4   not being herself. She looked like she wore a vinyl dress and
5   fishnet stockings every night of her life. The way she moved
6   her way through the crowd. Confident that they would part for
7   her. I just kept saying 'excuse me' in a voice that no one
8   could hear anyway. So I tried drinking. Three Long Island iced
9   teas and that somebody else has still not arrived. It's just me
10 here, just a slightly intoxicated me who's finding it quite
11 difficult to walk in high-heel platform shoes.
12   Now Jessie's making out with some guy and I'm sitting
13 here wondering what time it is. You know, it's funny 'cause,
14 even though it was her idea to dress up I think I was the one
15 who was more excited to be somebody else. Not that I hate
16 myself or anything. I just wanted to see what it would be like
17 for things to be ... easy. I guess pink feather boas can't do
18 everything.
19
20
21
22
23
24
25
26
27
28
29
30
31
32
33
34
35

The General of Hot Desire
by John Guare

1 Eve   Young Adult
2

3 *Inspired by William Shakespeare's sonnets 153 and 154, here is the*
4 *gloomy view of a contemporary biblical Eve recently developed in*
5 *a theatre project titled "Love's Fire" for The Acting Company of New*
6 *York City. In this new interpretation, Christ turns to Eve to help him*
7 *find the right words to define what he's trying to do in the world.*
8 *The sassy young Eve's response is fiery and feisty.*
9

10   The words? I'm still naming things? This damn tree. We
11 chop it down. We carve its wood. We eat its leaves,
12 constantly mistake knowledge for mercy — we keep
13 constantly taking from that tree — that's all we know. All
14 God knows how to do is expel us from Eden. Over and over.
15 All man knows is how to try to get back. Play on wooden
16 pipes. Sing songs — make a sonnet.
17   Ababcdcdefef gg.
18   Can fourteen lines bear so much weight?
19   The weight of auditioning for God?
20   Hoping this time He will hear us?
21   A symphony, a drawing, a dance, a sonnet.
22   These fragile inventions of man's are man's only defense
23 against the silence of God.
24   And we keep trying to contact that which cannot be
25 contacted, name that which cannot be named, define that
26 which can never be defined. What are our tools? Something
27 as paltry as a sonnet —
28   A song —
29   A dance —

1   A story —
2   Is a hazy reminder of what we had in that garden when the
3 Tree of Knowledge still grew alongside forests of mercy.
4   God, we wanted mercy and all you gave us was knowledge.
5
6
7
8
9
10
11
12
13
14
15
16
17
18
19
20
21
22
23
24
25
26
27
28
29
30
31
32
33
34
35

A Blue Streak
by Staci Swedeen

1   Missy   Adult

2

3   *Missy, a mature woman who thinks she is aging much too quickly,*
4   *enrolls in an exercise class to confront the ravages of time that she*
5   *imagines are overtaking her. She provides an intimate glimpse of*
6   *the personal trauma she is experiencing in this "aging thing." Her*
7   *outbursts, however, are more comic than serious and provide a nice*
8   *satirical point of view on exercise in general.*

9

10   I'm not taking this aging thing well. I always thought that
11   I would, that I'd be one of those smiling, super-fit, Jane
12   Fonda clones. Do you have any idea how many funky dance
13   classes you'd have to take to look like that? Do you? But I
14   keep trying because, hey, what's the alternative? Tomorrow's
15   my birthday. I know, thanks, I don't look it. Right. This
16   morning I woke up and I could smell my body rotting. Really,
17   I smelled it. Now, I'm not sick or anything, but I smelled this
18   sweet smell, dank, and it stuck in my throat. I knew that this
19   body that I'm in would one day be — I mean, I felt like I —
20   I'm decomposing. That, in fact, my body is already —
21   already — breaking down, just so subtley that most days I
22   don't notice.
23   If I keep busy I don't think about it so much. But I lost
24   interest in being in this body, you know what I mean? I just
25   thought, no — no, thank you, I don't want to experience
26   this. Oh, sometimes, sometimes, it's okay — like after
27   aerobics, or eating chocolate, but most of the time ... and I
28   don't want Jack to know. I'm afraid that he'll, he'll leave.
29   Wouldn't you? I can't tell him. I don't know how to tell him.

1   So I keep at it, buying new lipstick and taking tae bo. How do
2   you say to someone — have you noticed anything recently?
3   That I'm disintegrating? That you're making love to a corpse?
4
5
6
7
8
9
10
11
12
13
14
15
16
17
18
19
20
21
22
23
24
25
26
27
28
29
30
31
32
33
34
35

Random Women
by Carolyn Carpenter

1   Lucy   Teen/Young Adult

2

3   *Lucy, a famous pop star, has charmed the nation with her*

4   *inspired story of rising from poverty to stardom. She is an*

5   *American idol, oozing Southern charm and natural good looks*

6   *that make her every man's dream and every girl's best friend.*

7   *Standing on a blank stage warming up an imaginary audience*

8   *with a well-rehearsed speech, Lucy's cell phone rings and we*

9   *begin to see and hear a darker side of our idol.*

10

11   Howdy! Man, it's good to be here tonight. This is our

12 last city! Wow. What a ride. Travelling across the good ol'

13 U. S. of A! Let's hear it! Oh, yeah! I wrote this next song a

14 long time ago when I was livin' in a little shack outside

15 Shreveport, Louisiana. I don't know, somehow I was

16 inspired watchin' my mama scrape together that meal of

17 corn chowder with extra flour. She'd stare at it, as if her

18 glare was gonna turn it into an eight-course prime rib

19 dinner. Poor thing. I don't know how she did it. I actually

20 wore hand-me-downs from my five brothers. People thought

21 I was a boy until ... well ... you know. *(Blushes.)* But some of

22 those days were the greatest. Trompin' through the swamps

23 with the green mud squishin' through our toes. Just bein'

24 so alive together. I tell ya the first thing I did when my

25 album started selling was surprise my family with a limo

26 that took us to that eight-course prime rib dinner. Boy, that

27 was somethin'. Oh, I'm sorry for goin' on. I don't know how

28 I got to be so corny. Musta been the chowder. But corny is

29 good for writin' songs. *(Reacting to the crowd.)* Aw, you're too

1 kind. Really. Don't forget these guys, lurkin' behind me,
2 they're my band! Yeah, ain't they great? They take good care
3 of me. *(Strumming on her guitar.)* Oh, I just hate to play this
4 last song 'cuz then it'll all be over. And who knows when I'll
5 be in your town again? Who knows when? I'm just hopin' I
6 inspire you to go home and pick up your own instrument, even
7 if that instrument is just a pen. Write a few lines of poetry. A
8 few thoughts from your heart. You never know ...
9   *(A cell phone in her bag rings. Irritated, LUCY growls into the*
10 *phone.)* **Yeah?** *(Suddenly LUCY's accent vanishes. She isn't*
11 *speaking to an audience, she is watching herself in a mirror. She*
12 *adjusts her clothes in the reflection.)*
13   I'm rehearsing. How did you get this number? Yes, I'm
14 alone. Oh please, I don't want to waste my time on the band,
15 Mother. Give me a break. No, I'm not coming home. Because
16 I hate New England. Thanksgiving, what a hoax. You and
17 Sterling will have to get along without me. You know, I really
18 don't have time for this. And stop calling me Tiffany. It's Lucy
19 now, got it? Yeah. Whatever. *(She drops the cell phone into her*
20 *bag. Goes back to rehearsing. Giggles.)*
21   My name's Lucy. And this goes out to all the little people
22 that are dreamin' of bein' big!
23
24
25
26
27
28
29
30
31
32
33
34
35

nailing the books shut
by Steven A. Schutzman

1   Joy   Young Adult/Adult

2

3   *Joy, a mature woman, wants a child but her writer boyfriend,*
4   *Robert, just can't read between the lines. Over the years of their*
5   *relationship, the uneducated Joy has come to share Robert's love*
6   *of books. Since they can't now decide how to divide their books,*
7   *Robert, in a frenzy, has begun nailing the books shut with a*
8   *hammer. Joy, the street wise New Yorker, circles her prey as a*
9   *U-Haul waits outside for Robert's stuff.*

10

11   No. No. I'm not giving in. Not now. I give in, it's over for
12 me and I got this terrible ache, Bobby. So nail the books.
13 Go ahead. What do I care? 'Cause the books're in me now
14 like you are, and the next guy maybe won't be such a pig
15 about all he knows and I don't. Because I have it in me and
16 maybe he'll even feel wow, what an interesting mind she
17 has, not just the great bod you can't get enough of and
18 yeah and yeah and the late nights and the believing in you
19 and pulling you through 'til you finished your novel. *(Beat.)* I
20 can get more books, Bobby. You taught me to love books so
21 you might as well nail'em shut or whatever. Can't decide
22 what to do with stuff like our love then just throw it away.
23 The baby. Cut it in half, whatever. What's Jim say to Huck,
24 'What good's half a baby? I wouldn't give you a dollar for a
25 million of 'em.' Where's Huck Finn? Nail him shut next why
26 don't you? Go ahead. Nail Huck.

27

28

29

The Food Monologues
by Kerri Kochanski

1 Woman   Young Adult/Adult
2
3 *A deprived, overweight woman speaks to an unseen someone*
4 *who has a choice layer cake in hand. Although she admits she*
5 *should not be eating, the tasty temptation is simply irresistible*
6 *and the woman begins to twist logic and choke reason in order*
7 *to rationalize her need for a gourmet treat. The topic here is a*
8 *serious one, but the comic character is colorful and the point of*
9 *view is playful.*
10
11   Piece. I want a piece of it. If you would just give me a
12 piece. Not a whole piece or half-a-piece ... but just a little.
13 Yes, that's it ... a little sliver. Then I could feel calmer. Then
14 I could feel ... *(She searches for a word.)* **good.**
15   Not good like when you do something you're supposed
16 to do, because you know it's right, and you get this big
17 warm fuzzy feeling but because ... *(She takes the cake, puts it*
18 *in her mouth, and chews. Tastes the flavor. Begins to savor it*
19 *orgasmically.)*
20   Yes ... Yes ... Because there are pleasures in life. Pleah ...
21 zures. And people should really enjoy those pleasures —
22 before they die. Before they are *not able* to enjoy them
23 anymore. People have lips, people have mouths. God gave
24 us these lips and mouths so we could do something *with*
25 them. If we weren't supposed to *do* something, then He
26 wouldn't have *given* them. He gave us *stomachs*, too.
27 Stomachs for collecting *food.* Some of us have bigger
28 baskets than others. *Some* of us are bigger gatherers.
29   And there's nothing wrong with being a bigger gatherer.

1 It just proves ... it just proves ... *(She tries to think of*
2 *something. Finally getting it.)* **That we are** *better* **at it. We are**
3 **better gatherers. We are** *good* **at something. Better than those**
4 **skinny people. We don't need to be** *skinny* **people. Not when**
5 **God is relying on us to do His work. To fill His baskets. The**
6 **baskets that He made. If He didn't want us to have them, He**
7 **wouldn't have** *made* **them. He wouldn't have made** *food.* **He**
8 **wouldn't have made** *cake.* *(She re-decides.)*
9 **Why don't you just give me it all then? I mean, since it's**
10 **there. I mean, God wouldn't want you to waste it.** *(She begins*
11 *to argue.)* **You don't need it. Your basket is too small. You can't**
12 **carry ...** *(Confidently.)* **I can carry.** *I* **can carry that cake. I wear**
13 **it well.** *You* **don't wear it at all. We can't see it. So why bother?**
14
15
16
17
18
19
20
21
22
23
24
25
26
27
28
29
30
31
32
33
34
35

Sleeper from Atlanta
by Thomas M. Kelly

1 Sara   Adult
2
3 *Sara, a mature woman with an undiagnosed borderline*
4 *personality, has reached a point in her life from which she fears*
5 *she may never recover. Destroying the tenuous bond she had*
6 *with her children by beating them and shattering her marriage by*
7 *making insurmountable demands on her husband, Sara returns*
8 *home to Atlanta, Georgia, from New York and confides to her*
9 *lawyer friend, Luci, that her life is in shambles.*
10
11   You should have heard that fat cop when he stopped me
12 on 285. *(Mimicking the sheriff's deputy.)* 'Now, maim, we here
13 in DeKalb County, kinda laik ta keep traffic flowin', but
14 maim you were doin' ieighty when ah got behind ya. Ak'll be
15 needin' your reagistration and driver's laicense. Aaahh, ya'll
16 from New York. Ah'll be balk in a few minutes. Ya'll just
17 relax. Ah, maim, Ah notice yer kids ain't straiapped in thar.
18 Ah'm agoinna haive ta taiket ya fer that, too, maim.' You
19 were stopped for speeding, Luci. *(Exuberant, prolonged*
20 *laughter.)* Ha, ha, ha. I gave the copy of your driver's license.
21 I wanted to hurt you as much as you hurt me. I thought for
22 sure that if I could get you to come down here for Jacob's
23 birthday I could convince you to take my case. *(Pause.)*
24   The boys were so upset. Cranky. Crying. I came back to
25 the neighborhood and parked in their school lot. Just
26 around the corner. *(Pause.)* Jacob kept nagging me. He
27 wanted to play in the school playground. And Elias wanted
28 to go home. While we were on the road it was just a few
29 taps to remind them that I'm the mother. They wouldn't

1 stop whining and crying. I lost it, Luci. I began hitting them. I
2 slapped Jacob so hard that his face was red. His eyes were
3 swollen with tears. He was sobbing convulsively. I saw the
4 fear, the horror in my baby Elias' eyes. I hit him. And I kept
5 hitting him. For no reason. He just sat there. Didn't say a
6 word. Didn't even cry. Just the look of fright. Fear in his eyes.
7 He was afraid of me. Me. His mother. *(Pause.)*
8   When they wouldn't stop crying, I started whaling at them.
9 But they just wouldn't stop crying. Screaming. *(Pause.)* I was
10 beating them for being kids. I hit them harder. Harder and
11 harder until they stopped crying. When I looked at them, their
12 eyes were open wide, horrified at what I might do next. It was
13 me. Me! They were horrified of *me!* I was the monster! *(Pause.)*
14   My stepfather ... He said the same thing to Jimmy and
15 me. *(Deep male voice.)* 'You want something to cry about? I'll
16 give you something to cry about.' He was such a coward. He
17 didn't use his hands on me. He used his belt. Mom was
18 helpless for fear of getting beaten herself. Punishment for
19 Jimmy was different. He used his fists on Jimmy. Jimmy
20 never recovered. The scars are still there. In prison you get to
21 choose your visitors. He refuses. *(Pause.)*
22   I had a beautiful family with Edgar. Destroyed that one and
23 moved on to the next, and the next. I seem to find fault with
24 everyone. One job after another. I blame everyone else for my
25 failures. I abused them. Even you. I stole from you. My best, the
26 only, friend I have left. *(Pause.)* Now, I've lost my babies. *(Pause.)*
27 Did you see them cowering in fear? Jacob was so afraid of me
28 his whole body was shaking. He threw up all over himself. Will
29 my children ever trust me again? Oh, my God. I've lost them.
30 *(Weeping, SARA raises her head quickly and breaks away from LUCI.)*
31   Is Jerry still here? He hasn't left yet, has he? I've lost him,
32 too. Another marriage down the tubes. He'll be gone soon. If
33 he's not gone already. He's really a very good man. *(Pause.)* I
34 can't go on like this! *(She collapses into LUCI's arms again,*
35 *sobbing uncontrollably.)*

Turnaround
by Clem Martini and Cheryl Foggo

1 Megan   Youthful/Teen
2
3 *Megan, a young adolescent, stands before a judge to request a*
4 *legal separation from her mother. She reveals the shocking events*
5 *that brought her not only to a turning point in her life but also to*
6 *this extreme legal court action. Megan's sense of maturity and*
7 *personal strength is remarkable for her age, and her plea for*
8 *happiness and individual fulfillment is very persuasive.*
9
10   The last time I saw my mother she was thin and curled
11 up in a ball, eyes rolled back in her head. I called 911 and
12 they took her away, and when the ambulance picked her up
13 the only thing I knew for sure was I was on my way to
14 somewhere else. Again. She'd been home from detox for
15 about two weeks and she promised things were going to be
16 different. And at first they were. Different. She came to a
17 parent/teacher interview. We went for a walk one time, down
18 to the river.
19   Then I walked in the door after school one day and there
20 was ... and I was afraid to even touch her. I stood in the
21 doorway saying, 'Mommy.' I called the ambulance, and it
22 took her away and after I was so ... angry. At me. I mean,
23 how could I have been so stupid? How could I have fallen for
24 that? *(Beat.)*
25   I've never lived anywhere. I've always been on my way
26 somewhere else, to the next place. Till now. I been at the
27 same place for a year — almost a year. I've been in trouble
28 in the past, but I'm not causing any trouble now. I'm
29 minding my own business. I'm not on any honor roll at

1 school, but I'm doing better than I ever have. I've spent more
2 time away from my mother than with her. She thinks I love
3 her, but I don't know what that means. I don't even know her
4 anymore. She says give her a chance, but what I want to know
5 is, and what I want someone, someone, to tell me is, how
6 many chances does she get to ruin my life?
7
8
9
10
11
12
13
14
15
16
17
18
19
20
21
22
23
24
25
26
27
28
29
30
31
32
33
34
35

Life
by Amy Bryan

1   Kim   Young Adult/Adult

2

3   *Kim, a troubled young woman who questions her own sanity at*
4   *times, is preparing to end her life. Sitting in a chair Center Stage, she*
5   *gets up after a pause and walks to the edge of the stage and begins*
6   *to titter as if she were on the ledge of a rooftop. As she calmly*
7   *begins to reflect on her farewell to life, however, Kim's view of the*
8   *inevitable reality of death leads to an unexpected self-realization.*

9

10   People laugh. All my life they have laughed at me. It
11 might have been my height, or my clothes, or my glasses.
12 But whatever it was, they always laughed. It's cold up here,
13 and windy. I wonder if it will hurt when I hit the pavement.
14 People jump everyday, right? It's no big thing! It can't be all
15 that bad. *(Trying to convince herself.)* It can't be that bad. I
16 was never sure of what I wanted in life. I felt I was always in
17 the cold, in some dark hole that only became deeper as I
18 got older. The first attempt was at sixteen, but half way
19 through I realized what a horrible mistake it would be, so I
20 decided it wasn't worth it. When I was eighteen I decided to
21 go to college, but then things took a turn for the worst.
22 Everything I saw was a way of escape. If I went to the beach
23 I felt it would be a luxury to just walk into the water, and
24 keep walking forever. If I was at a bonfire, I somehow knew
25 that the burn could not be as painful as life can be. Pills I
26 thought I would be able to take like candies, even a gun
27 would seem to relieve some pain.

28   But as life kept on going, I realized that I never would do
29 it! Why could I never do it? What possible reason could I

1 have for not ending my pain and misery? Well the games are
2 over, now I am going to do it. *(She looks over the edge of the*
3 *stage.)* Wait. No. There is something that keeps me here. Even
4 through the pain and suffering, I never did it because I wasn't
5 meant to, because someone is keeping me here. I am here for
6 a reason. If I never had the nerve to do it, it's because
7 someone's will for me to stay on this earth is stronger than my
8 will to leave it. I know the meaning of life, and maybe if I jump,
9 they would laugh at me. I won't let it happen. Maybe life can
10 be as good as I want it to be. *(Slowly moves away from the edge*
11 *of the stage and returns to her seat.)*
12
13
14
15
16
17
18
19
20
21
22
23
24
25
26
27
28
29
30
31
32
33
34
35

Inside a Seashell
by Deborah Castellano

1   Leah   Teen/Young Adult

2

3   *Leah, a lonely figure dressed in pajamas, is a young woman*
4   *recently assaulted by one of her male friends. Pacing the floor late*
5   *at night, she is talking to her sister, Emily, who is in an adjoining*
6   *bedroom. This is the first time Leah has spoken of the assault,*
7   *and she is consumed with feelings of self-doubt and inadequacy*
8   *in the struggle to understand what has happened to her.*

9

10   Michael wasn't supposed to be one of the bad guys. It's
11 my own fault anyway. Drank too much ... wore that short
12 skirt ... sat on his lap, flirting with him. I didn't expect ...
13 Everything happened so fast. It's all just a blur, like a
14 picture taken too soon. I was on my back. He was ... Peter
15 pulled him off me. I just laughed, made a joke. Went into
16 the bathroom, threw up in my hair. Sat on the cold tile floor
17 and cried for an hour. But all you could see is that I didn't
18 Do the Right Thing. Didn't press charges. Didn't go to the
19 police or hospital. You asked if I said no. If I said no. Of
20 course I said no! Not that it mattered when he's so much
21 bigger than I am. As if I wanted this to happen to me. I felt
22 like he was thrusting a jagged glass bottle into me. All I
23 could think of was the ocean. And how I felt like I was
24 trapped inside a seashell, where all I could hear was the
25 sound of the tides. I didn't want him slobbering all over me.
26 Bruises on my breasts. If you would only stop asking about
27 it, I could pretend this didn't happen. I could make it go
28 away. I just ... want it to go away.

29

Flipping Over Red
by Beverly Rees

1   Deirdre   Youthful/Teen

2

3   *Deirdre (Deedee) is an innocent young girl experiencing the*
4   *awakening hint of an attraction to the opposite sex. Wrestling*
5   *with anxiety and self-doubt, Deirdre is unintentionally confronted*
6   *with questions about infatuation, the true nature of love, and*
7   *intimacy. Here, she tries to answer these puzzling riddles with a*
8   *sense of honesty and humor.*

9

10   When I was in the eighth grade I had the misfortune to
11 be hopelessly in love with Red. My mother did not approve
12 of him. He was sixteen and had quit school right after
13 Christmas, and he hung around with a much older guy who
14 lived across the street, and my mother viewed the whole
15 set-up as somehow unsavory.
16   I knew I was in love the day Mr. Gravino decided to teach
17 us to do forward hand springs. I had to run to Red, put my
18 hands on his knees and he flipped me over his head — and I
19 felt like I could be happy flipping over Red forever. My
20 mother never found out about the time I went with him to
21 the barn behind his house. Several bales of straw were piled
22 up table high, and I found myself leaning back against them,
23 Red kissing me on the mouth, kissing me gently, sweetly,
24 long — causing new, strange, and wonderful sensations to
25 quiver right through me. I was not in the least afraid, my
26 mind just seemed to shut down — yielding only to the
27 moment and Red whispering, please, please — his body
28 leaning hard against me. Then suddenly he was pulling me
29 to my feet, and we walked down Rue Avenue, neither of us

1 having much to say, and at my corner he said, 'See ya,' and I
2 said, 'See ya' — and you see, the bad thing is — my mother
3 thought I had gone to Youth Fellowship with Bonnie.
4   The whole thing came to a terrible end one night when I
5 let Red in — when my parents were out. And honestly, he
6 never did me any harm whatsoever — we just sat there on the
7 porch in silence, each one of us rocking in one of the rockers,
8 and my father came home unexpectedly — and he was
9 furious. He told him if he didn't stay away from me he'd break
10 his neck. Naturally he avoided me after that, and for awhile I
11 hated my father. One night, not long after, Dorrie and I spent
12 the night at my grandmother's house. As we walked to the
13 boardwalk we noticed a carnival in full swing on the municipal
14 parking lot. It wasn't long before my ever-wandering eyes
15 focused on Red operating the Ferris wheel.
16   I dragged Dorrie over to buy tickets and while we were
17 standing in line, he walked over and handed Dorrie a whole
18 strip of tickets — never saying one word or even glancing my
19 way. Round and round we went, me watching that flaming hair
20 — my misery increasing with each new turn. I made Dorrie
21 hang around for a long time afterward, praying he'd come over
22 but he never did. Crossing the shadowy parking lot we spotted
23 two large photographs lying on the ground. We gaped head to
24 head, amazed, and thoroughly shocked. Each one showed a
25 nude man and a nude woman in the most bizarre positions
26 imaginable in glossy black and white. Were ordinary people
27 supposed to perform like this we wondered, my parents, her
28 parents, anybody's parents? We quickly concluded it couldn't
29 possibly be and we tore them into tiny pieces and threw them
30 in a storm sewer — but the hapless images were indelible.
31
32
33
34
35

The Search for Signs of Intelligent Life in the Universe
by Jane Wagner

1 Agnus Angst   Teen/Young Adult

2

3 *Originally written as a one-woman tour de force for the*
4 *comedienne Lily Tomlin — who played all of the roles — this*
5 *satirical narrative features Agnus Angst, a fifteen-year-old rebel*
6 *who has locked herself in the ladies' room of the International*
7 *House of Pancakes. Here, the neurotic self-dramatizer wails her*
8 *sob story of shattered dreams and paranoid fears in a phone call*
9 *to a local radio shrink.*

10

11   Hello, Charlotte, listen, it is *vital* I stay over at your
12 house tonight!

13   Don't ask me to explain.

14   You've got to make your mom let me stay over!

15   Can't you force her to say yes?

16   Look, my parents think you're a bad influence on me,
17 too.

18   Just for that, you can't run the equipment at my gig
19 tonight.

20   You are out of my life, Charlotte; you are *her*story. You
21 are the 'crumb de la crumb.'

22   Drop off my tape at the Un-Club, or I'll sue you for all
23 you're worth.

24   It is vital, Charlotte.

25   Don't you eyeball me, you *speck*! Can't you see I am
26 *using* this *phone!*

27   And don't you *touch* that cage.

28

1   That's my parakeet in there.

2   Hello?

3   Look it's vital I talk to the radio shrink. My name's Agnus.

4   I'm fifteen. My *parents* locked me out of the house today.

5   I want to find out if that is *legal.*

6   I'm in the ladies' room, House of Pancakes.

7   I can't wait long.

8   Hello? Is this Dr. Kassorla, the psychologist?

9   Look, Doctor, for years I've been going home after school,
10   nobody would be there —

11   I'd take my key from around my neck and let myself in.

12   But today I go home, I put my key in the door ...

13   *They changed the locks on me!*

14   Yeah, maybe it *was* something I did. I didn't say I was
15   innocent.

16   Whatever I do is wrong, anyway. Like, last night, my
17   stepmom, she accuses me of leaving dirty fingerprints on the
18   *cheese.*Even getting an innocent piece of cheese becomes a
19   criminal act.

20   But the problem goes deeper: my real mother's not around
21   much right now.

22   She's in Europe, Germany or someplace, doing her art
23   thing.

24   She's a performance artist. Like me.

25   There was this big custody beef, see, 'cause my real
26   mother's a lesbian.

27   So the court gave me to my dad.

28   He's a gene-splicer, a bio-businessman at this research
29   lab of misapplied science.

30   Where he's working on some new bio-form he thinks he'll
31   be able to patent.

32   He doesn't get that I am a new bio-form.

33   *I am using this phone!* You IHOP speck!

34   So today I go to my dad's lab, to get some money for some
35   gear for my act, and I see this glob of bio-plasm quivering

1 there in this petri dish.
2   I don't know why I did it.
3   Maybe it was sibling rivalry.
4   But I leaned over and I spit into it.
5   And of course, my dad had a *mad scientist alert!*
6   He says I've ruined years of research.
7   The truth is he loves that *bio-form* more than *me*.
8   Yeah, I thought of calling the hot line for runaways, but I'm
9 worried maybe they don't take throwaways like me.
10   I have other family, my grandparents, but we have nothing
11 in common, except that we are all carbon-based life forms.
12   What?
13   A commercial?
14   I can't believe you're brushing me off.
15   To sell some product that probably killed some poor *lab rat*.
16   *You've been about as helpful as an acid FLASHBACK!*
17   *Hey, where's my parakeet? Conway Tweety!*
18   *THAT CREEP! STOLE MY PARAKEET!*
19   Hey, you IHOP specks, you *must* have seen somebody
20 leave with a cage.
21   You all saw me come in with one.
22   Don't you stare at me with those *blueberry syrup*
23 *mustaches!*
24
25
26
27
28
29
30
31
32
33
34
35

Dental Mania
by Ludmilla Bollow

1 Bride   Young Adult
2
3 *A young woman, dressed in a fancy wedding gown splattered*
4 *with blood, rushes into a decrepit dental office in excruciating*
5 *pain! The hysterical soon-to-be bride covers her bleeding mouth*
6 *with a fist and collapses into a chair. There is an air of anxiety*
7 *that surrounds her as she spins a tale of disappointment and*
8 *misery for the amusement of the stunned listeners.*
9
10   **Where's the damn dentist! I need to see the dentist! Fast!**
11   *(Listens, then points finger at patient in chair.)* **What do you**
12 **mean, I have to take a number? I have to wait my turn? Not**
13 **today, lady! I've been waiting my turn all my life for this day.**
14 **Then, then, on the way to church, this maniac taxi driver,**
15 **he takes a short cut through this nowhere land, hitting the**
16 **bumps like crazy — so I'll get there on time — so the groom**
17 **doesn't have a chance to escape. This taxi guy's yakking on**
18 **and on, when wham! He smacks into this mountaintop of a**
19 **bump, and bam! I break off my tooth — right in the front of**
20 **my big mouth!** *(Opens mouth, pointing.)*
21   **Blood! Blood all over my beautiful wedding dress too!**
22 **Look at me! I'm a mess. A complete horrible mess. On the**
23 **one day I should be looking my most gorgeous!** *(Sits.)* **All I**
24 **need is something temporary to fill up this hideous gap. Or**
25 **the dentist to nail the old tooth back in. Whatever. So when**
26 **I march down that aisle, and pull my veil aside, I don't look**
27 **like some fugitive from a horror show ... I don't want any**
28 **photos of me looking like this either!** *(Rises with new wailing.)*
29 **I dreamed of this day since I was a little girl — getting**

1 married — the most special day of my life, and already it's
2 turned into a big pile of stinking ... Where's that dentist?
3 *(Looks and points at patient.)* What garbage are you babbling
4 about now? Is this a dentist's office, or not? The sign says
5 'Take number'? What do you mean, take a number? *(New*
6 *rage.)* You wanta give me another number, do you? Whack
7 another number onto me, besides all those I already got. I'm
8 plastered with numbers — my wallet can't hold anymore.
9 Social Security. Blue Cross. *(Goes faster and faster.)* Driver's
10 license, phone numbers, access codes, locker numbers,
11 internet addresses — Numbers! Numbers! AAGH! Besides the
12 numbers I have to carry to tell me who I am, besides that, all
13 day long I punch in stupid numbers on the computer at that
14 crummy bank! All day long I attack numbers — they attack
15 me back — follow me, even into my sleep! *(Screaming out.)*
16 I don't want another number! Not on this red letter day!
17 This was the one day I wanted to escape from the number
18 world, fly off into fairytale land with my Barney. *(Pause.)*
19 Barney's not into numbers — he's into body-building. Well,
20 sometimes he counts his barbell lifts — or how many beers
21 he's downed. *(Looks at watch.)* He'll think I backed out. I was
22 telling him last night, I wasn't so sure about going through
23 with this. All our differences. Our fights. But, nobody else has
24 ever asked me to marry them before. Hey, I'm not going to
25 turn down my one and only chance to walk down that aisle,
26 looking like a fairy princess. That's all I ever wanted — one
27 day — one dream to come true. Then, then, this stupid idiot,
28 this part-time taxi driver ... *(Rises, looks in a mirror.)*
29 My mouth hurts. My hair's drooping — and my beautiful
30 dress, smeared in blood! I'll never pull myself together in time.
31 Ruined! My whole life is ruined! *(Pounds fist on coffee table. Starts*
32 *throwing magazines around in a rage. Stops and looks up. New*
33 *rage.)* You! Mad Max, the reckless taxi driver! *(Beat.)* You want
34 to know if I still want to go to the church or not? Don't come
35 near me — or I'll tear your eyes out! Driving like a maniac —

1 through this forsaken part of town! How can I go to the church
2 now? You tell me! Looking like a refugee from hell! You're
3 lucky if you even get your fare, or that I don't sue for damages!
4 *(Beat.)* **What do you mean, you can help me! You helped me**
5 **enough already.** *(Pause.)*
6   You say you could help me with a lawsuit, because you're
7 studying to be a lawyer? You only drive a taxi part-time. *(Beat.)*
8 The guy I'm marrying, Barney — he didn't even finish high
9 school. I pick the first simp what comes along — because he
10 has a muscular build. Didn't even look past his body, see if
11 there were any brains lingering inside that chunk of muscle. I
12 figured, after I married him — I could maybe wisen him up
13 some ... send him off to school. Still hurts ... *(Pause.)* **What's**
14 **that you're saying? You want me to come home with you?**
15 You'll wash the blood off my dress. You have some crazy glue,
16 and can try gluing my tooth back in, or use some white
17 modeling clay to fill up the hole. Then — then — we can go
18 back to the wedding. *(Walks about a bit.)*
19   I don't know — if he'll wait for me. Barney, he's so
20 impatient — doesn't like to wait for anything. He has such a
21 huge temper. Sometimes he can get so ugly. You want me to
22 call the church. Tell them there was an accident.
23 *(Retrospective.)* **He didn't want to get married anyway. Says I**
24 **sucked him into it.** Didn't want to 'march down that aisle in a
25 stupid monkey suit — have a ball and chain attached to him
26 for the rest of his life.' He won't wait for me. *(Wails.)*
27   Do I love him? I don't know. I thought I might — someday.
28 *(Hand to mouth in pain.)* **Know what? I think I'll skip my**
29 **wedding for today.** No way can I go through with it anymore.
30 Not now, not in the state I'm in. Maybe you and your terrible
31 driving is just what I needed to save me from a fate worse
32 than hell. Let's go — to your house, and maybe I can start all
33 over again. **Maybe with someone with brains.** *(Exits trilling.)*
34 Here goes the bride ...
35

A Woman on the Moon
by Edward Crosby Wells

1   Gloria and Betty   Adults

2

3   *Duolog*

4   *There is a hint of "black comedy" in this duolog that*

5   *features two mature women calmly engaged in everyday*

6   *polite conversation while enjoying an afternoon lunch at a*

7   *restaurant. The women exchange clichéd sentiments and*

8   *trite pleasantries to mask a very human — and comic — view*

9   *of life that may have temporarily lost its meaning. The*

10   *characters — perhaps rather late in life — appear to be*

11   *rebellious as they wrestle with trivial questions that now*

12   *appear to be of major significance in their lives. The wry, far-*

13   *fetched point of view expressed here is subtly satiric with*

14   *brightly humorous lines and sharply drawn banter that is*

15   *sure to provoke laughter. In playing the scene you will need*

16   *to be inventive in bodily actions, gestures, and reactions to*

17   *highlight the responses of characters who are confined to*

18   *chairs. The novelty of this scene should encourage*

19   *imaginative use of pauses, facial expressions, and peculiar*

20   *mannerisms to flesh out the character portraits.*

21

22   *Gloria and Betty, two mature, middle-class women, are*

23   *seated at a table tallying the check from their luncheon.*

24   *There is very little distinction suggested in each woman's*

25   *attitude or mood — indeed, these characters might be seen*

26   *as two sides of the same personality. Although their*

27   *behavior is calm and civil, there is an explosive undertone*

28   *that threatens to burst forth at the slightest provocation.*

29

1   GLORIA: Did you watch the moon landing the other day,
2   Betty?
3   BETTY: No, Gloria. I didn't care to see a man lay claim to yet
4   one more piece of real estate. You had the fruit salad.
5   Men already think they own the world ... and now they've
6   got to have the moon, too. I had the three-bean soup.
7   'One small step for man; one giant leap for Mankind.'
8   Give me a break! I wonder who wrote that bit of
9   misogyny? Sixty-cents for the soup. That's mine. Do you
10   know why they didn't send a woman to the moon?
11   Seventy-five cents for the fruit salad. That's yours.
12   GLORIA: No, why is that?
13   BETTY: Imagine how those men in Washington would react to
14   hearing, 'One small step for woman...?'
15   GLORIA: They'd freak.
16   BETTY: You bet they'd freak. Egg salad sandwich, ninety-
17   cents. That's mine. One day it will be our turn. Fried
18   bologna on rye, seventy-five cents. That's yours. One day
19   there will be a woman on the moon. That will be a day to
20   celebrate.
21   GLORIA: I'd be happy to get to Las Vegas one day. Too many
22   seeds in the rye and he never did bring the horseradish.
23   My bra is killing me. I think I'm going to buy one of those
24   living bras.
25   BETTY: What?
26   GLORIA: Yeah, it's called a living bra and it's supposed to
27   hold you gently but firmly — like it had a mind of its own.
28   BETTY: Now, isn't that just what I need — something with a
29   mind of its own holding up my euphemisms. The side
30   order of slaw was forty-cents. That's yours.
31   GLORIA: But you ate it.
32   BETTY: Okay, we'll split it. Twenty-cents you owe and
33   twenty-cents I owe. One hot tea with lemon, a quarter.
34   That's mine. One day I'd like to burn mine.
35   GLORIA: Burn your what, your tea?

1 BETTY: My bra, Betty. One day I'd like to burn my bra.
2 GLORIA: Why?
3 BETTY: Gloria, do men wear bras?
4 GLORIA: No, not even when they obviously need them.
5 BETTY: Well, that's my point! One coffee, black. That's
6   yours. Twenty-five cents. So, what's in Las Vegas?
7 GLORIA: Huh?
8 BETTY: You said you wanted to go to Las Vegas. You do know
9   that women are enslaved in Las Vegas, don't you? The
10   fruit cup was mine — forty-cents. Haven't you ever heard
11   of showgirls?
12 GLORIA: Sure. I wanted to be a showgirl when I was a little girl.
13 BETTY: That's like wanting to be a performing dog!
14 GLORIA: It's not the same thing!
15 BETTY: It certainly is! Miss Gloria Steinem, the show dog!
16 GLORIA: Don't call me that! I hate it! Miss implies that there
17   is a man lacking in my life. How much was the rice
18   pudding, Miss Friedan?
19 BETTY: Sixty-cents! Don't change the subject!
20
21
22
23
24
25
26
27
28
29
30
31
32
33
34
35

Chapter V
The Gilded Age

Carve not upon a stone when I am dead
The praises which remorseful mourners give
To women's graves — a tardy recompense —
But speak them while I live.

— *Elizabeth Akers Allen,* Till Death

The monolog characters of the gilded age are also drawn from the everyday world, but they are more eccentric, flamboyant, or neurotic. They are bright, attractive characters with a comic flair that masks the outrageous behavior or emotional and psychological phobias that color their lives. These are very complex character portraits of stage figures who may be the products of inhibited heredity, deprived environment, failed relationships, or subconscious inhibitions that have left them with a distorted view of the world.

Because they are helplessly adrift in a world that has no apparent meaning or purpose for them, gilded characters choose to live in their own world and create their own set of values. In this "alien" world, the characters often struggle to establish meaningful relationships with other human beings or to regain a lost sense of self-identity. Although bewildered and frightened at times, the characters become increasingly more independent in both action and attitude. It is probably easier to understand the action and attitude of gilded characters by not thinking too much, and focusing on the obvious broad humor, comic flair, or eccentricity of these fickle stage figures.

In playing these monologs you should be concerned with capturing the outrageous spirit of good fun or misadventure of characters who take themselves much too seriously at times. Concentrate on developing a distinctive character voice and engage in active "word play" to underscore and highlight the humor of the dialog. Pay particular attention to gestures, mannerisms, movement, or personal habits that may give a more human personality to the character portraits here. Remember not to exaggerate to the extreme or the audience may find it difficult to recognize such obscure character portraits in their own life experience.

Aisle 12-B, Sundries
by Dinah L. Leavitt

1   Rose   Adult

2

3   *Rose, an elderly and widowed woman, stands impeccably*
4   *dressed in the aisle of the supermarket with her shopping cart.*
5   *She has created a social survival environment here and is a*
6   *regular customer. Through the lens of her make-believe world at*
7   *the Food King, Rose laments the downward slide of civilization*
8   *from a more genteel time when ladies were ladies, children were*
9   *quiet, and food wasn't junk.*

10

11   I always wear a girdle to the Food King. I'm glad they're
12   back — girdles. Oh now they call them body shapers and
13   they make them out of lycra, not rubber. I don't want to
14   jiggle when I walk in the aisle. People who know me, I know
15   everybody at the Food King, are often behind me. I want to
16   glide like my grocery cart. If I get a cart with a gimpy wheel,
17   I trade it in right away. Don't you?
18   It's so beautiful here. 'Clean and well-lighted.' I feel at
19   peace here. I remember Mr. Khayat's market when I was a
20   girl. Dark, dark and the meat section smelled. And they
21   didn't sell any of the nice things they sell here like candles,
22   reading glasses, tiger balm.
23   Creamettes are up three cents.
24   But in the old days you dressed to shop! Oh not hats
25   and gloves, but you wore a clean ironed dress. Lady shoes.
26   Now I see the most awful side of humanity. Started out
27   with the curlers in the 1950s. Pink and green mixed,
28   sometimes without even a scarf over them. Not even all the
29   same color ... Now it's athletic wear, that or blue jeans. No

1 self-respect. And I tell you I know some of these people are
2 not athletic. Look at them; they look awful!
3   Now and then somebody comes in from the old days and
4 I follow them. They never know I do it 'cause I switch
5 directions in the aisles or skip soda and chips. That way I can
6 see them coming and going — admire the besom on their
7 jacket pocket or their clicky patent heels, hair cut.
8   And what most people today buy! Junk, junk, junk. You
9 know you are what you eat and that's not just an old saying.
10 Look! *(Points to another cart.)* Fritos, Nature Valley granola bars —
11 the second ingredient is sugar, Skippy Peanut Butter, Sugar
12 Pops, and yogurt — read the label — half sugar! Microwave
13 popcorn, Kraft singles, Sara Lee — grease and sugar. It's all
14 grease and sugar and so are these people. It's sinful. Their
15 kids are, too. Little fatties.
16   Oh don't get me started on grocery store children. *Brats.* I
17 am sorry but 99% of them are brats pure unadulterated. The
18 good ones must stay at home. Whine, cry and fight the whole
19 time. Yesterday I saw a young boy roll a loaded cart over his
20 little sister's leg. Deliberately. Oh don't get me started. And
21 the checkout. Have to have every piece of junk up there.
22 Lifesavers, gum, artificially flavored juice in those waxy
23 container bottles. Squeezits! One boy went into hysterics
24 yesterday because his mama wouldn't let him have a copy of
25 *Better Homes and Gardens.* He wasn't old enough to read. My
26 mama would have popped me one good. She didn't buy him
27 the *Better Homes* but I say it's too late by the time they get to
28 the point of public tantrums at the checkout. Brats. I was
29 trapped in the checkout line with more than ten items so I
30 couldn't change to Express.
31   That's Mr. Thornhill. He's the manager; he knows me.
32 Since I reported the cigarette thief he knows my name. 'Hello,
33 Mrs. Rose,' he says. You'll hear him when he notices me. A
34 man was stealing a carton of Kools. If it had been a frozen
35 meat pie I would have thought twice but KOOLS. And I have

1   to pay for the shoplifters in higher prices throughout the store.
2   Even with EDLPs, coupons, TPRs, and specials, things cost. I
3   watch now. May God let this place be safe from thieves.
4   HiDry paper towels are two rolls for a dollar.
5   There's Grady Parker, he's vegetables. Joe Marino, meat,
6   Pat Leavy does the flowers — she says she isn't Jewish. Mike,
7   the boy with palsy, says he got a raise on Wednesday. I know
8   all the delivery schedules by heart and he loves to hear me
9   rattle them off. This is Sunday morning so there won't be any
10 deliveries until eleven thirty.
11   I wouldn't say we're all friendly; we don't visit outside the
12 grocery store, but in a way, we are like a family. I shop every
13 day. I love it here. If Jesus came back I think He'd be a stock
14 boy not a carpenter. Mr. Parker in vegetables always
15 comments on all the mouths I must have to feed. I just smile.
16 This is the only mouth I feed. Been alone for sixteen years. As
17 long as I have the Food King, I'm not lonely. I was 'til I started
18 coming every day, but if you come every day you see
19 everybody — everybody has to eat. A lot of ladies go to the
20 shopping mall, but I like this better. It's of a higher order. It's
21 food.
22   Listen, they're playing "Paper Moon." *(She hums the*
23 *melody.)* The music here is such a lift. Sometimes I dance
24 down the aisles. This would be a foxtrot, of course. *(ROSE*
25 *begins to sing the song and to sway as the lights fade to black.)*
26 'It's only a paper moon, adrift on a cardboard sea. But it
27 wouldn't be make believe ...'
28
29
30
31
32
33
34
35

Baby's in Black
by Frank Mancino

1 Julie   Adult
2
3 *Julie, a mature and cosmopolitan woman living in New York*
4 *City, has one hand in the arts and the other in technology. For*
5 *her birthday, she throws a party and is pressed to reveal why she*
6 *has not been able to commit to a meaningful relationship. Julie*
7 *tries to explain the source of the problem, her previous lover, and*
8 *delights the party guests with the humorous tale of "Art the Rat."*
9
10   Do you really want to know about Art the Rat? Okay, I
11 will tell you how he got that name. You know, and I hope you
12 won't take this personally, the thing that really bothers me
13 about men is the way they look at you when you first meet:
14 the head goes up, like a hound that has the scent; the
15 eyebrows lift; and sometimes the ears lay back a bit. Then
16 the eyes start travelling all over you, just to make sure they
17 recognize you later, say when you meet on the street, and
18 they are with someone else, and need to start laying plans
19 on — either avoiding you or pretending they hardly know
20 you, if they cannot avoid you entirely.
21   You know the 'well, how are you?' to cover the time
22 when they search for your name to introduce you to their
23 latest interest. Most of the time, I don't care if they
24 remember my name or not, and I would just as soon be
25 passed by, but now and then, there is one who should have
26 stopped ... You know and I know that most men are dogs,
27 but dogs are o.k. in my book. When we are teens, we all like
28 the purebreds: the Afghans, Collies, and even some of us go
29 for the Dobermans (but let's not go there, please). Then we

1   go through the mutt phase where the street dog is the love of
2   our life. Some of us marry the mutt, and some don't. I didn't,
3   but that doesn't mean I would not have, if things had turned
4   out differently.
5   But there are mutts and then there are rats, and Art is
6   definitely the latter. It was my birthday, the one day I wanted
7   to have things just right. It started out fine: we got up, had
8   breakfast, and were going to go to his baseball game, the
9   Wharf Rats vs. the Uptown Mob. So, what does Art do? He
10 picks a fight with me over some silly thing that I did, then
11 throws me out of the apartment, his apartment. So, the same
12 day, I go back to New Jersey, to the Melody Farm, and what
13 do I see when I open the door? A rat, dead on the bathroom
14 floor, expired from loneliness, I guess. So there we are, me
15 and the rat. I looked at the rat, and I thought about it. Now
16 Melody Farms always had a lot of stuff around, and I found a
17 box of English Leather. You remember how some guys always
18 loved English Leather, and it came in that little wooden box?
19 Yeah, and it is just the right size for a dead rat.
20   I had Art's team pin on, the one that said, 'Let's Go Wharf
21 Rats: Hit Another Homer!' — using my old Girl Scout swap-
22 making expertise, staying up half the night to get them just
23 right. So, I stuck that pin right between that rat's paws. He
24 was lying so peaceful in that box, and I sprinkled the English
25 Leather over him, and muttered my favorite incantation,
26 'that'll teach you to mess with this Gen Ex'er,' wrapped the
27 box in paper, and mailed it to Art's address, on Bank Street.
28 You know how long mail takes in New York? In the summer? I
29 figured that would certainly end things between us ... Was I
30 wrong! And though ending it was a lot easier after I met you,
31 I still cannot get over Art's ruining my birthday then, and the
32 next one too! And I swore that no one would mess with me on
33 that day ...
34
35

Betty's Summer Vacation
by Christopher Durang

1 Mrs. Siezmagraff   Adult
2
3 *Mrs. Siezmagraff (read* seismograph*), a bigger-than-life woman of*
4 *considerable social standing on the summer resort circuit,*
5 *encounters a derelict flasher in the women's changing room at*
6 *the beach. The naive Mrs. Siezmagraff invites the derelict back to*
7 *her vacation home and prepares to go out on a date with the*
8 *peeping tom. Here, she chats idly with another guest, the hapless*
9 *and forlorn Betty.*
10
11 *(To BETTY)* I have these enormous red welts on my upper
12 thighs. It's really unfortunate. I guess if I have sexual relations
13 with Mr. Vanislaw, we better keep the lights off. Or he could
14 be blindfolded, I guess. I've never done that, but people find it
15 exciting, I'm told. *(Checking what BETTY is cooking; or nibbling*
16 *on something.)* I once saw this movie about a sorority hazing,
17 and they showed these freshman girls this bowl of wiggling
18 worms, then they blindfolded them and fed them what they
19 assumed was the worms, but it was really just spaghetti, but
20 the girls didn't know that and they choked and vomited and
21 just had a terrible time ... I have no idea what the movie was.
22 I think that was the only scene of it I saw. It seemed to be
23 from the fifties. I think the difference between the innocence
24 of then versus now is that now they'd just go ahead and feed
25 them the worms and not bother about switching to spaghetti.
26 Isn't that sad? I feel something's been lost. But, oh well, we
27 have someone coming to dinner, so I shouldn't let my feelings
28 plummet down to the cellar, should I? La dee dah, oh for the
29 life of a swan. Is that the saying? Oh, for the life of something.

The Drunk Monologues
by Diane Spodarek

1 Woman   Young Adult/Adult
2
3 *An unnamed woman stands at the corner of 14th Street in New*
4 *York City and voices her view on the meaning of life to passers-*
5 *by during the rush hour. She appears to be on the verge of being*
6 *homeless and carries several plastic bags filled with clothes and*
7 *mementos. Although the woman at first glance resembles a*
8 *typical big city "bag lady," she has a simple dignity and wisdom*
9 *that sets her apart from other street people.*
10
11   You ever wonder why pigeons stay in New York? They
12 could fly anywhere couldn't they? If I had wings, I wouldn't
13 be standing here at this bus stop right now. I'd fly over to
14 Central Park or go by the water, you know? Maybe pigeons
15 are just like people, you know like New Yorkers, they can't
16 get the rhythm of the city out of their system. You ever
17 know someone who moves to California and then they come
18 back to New York? Maybe pigeons are just like that.
19 *(Walking around like a pigeon.)*
20   Hey Horace. I thought you were in San Francisco? Hey
21 Milt, good to see you. Yep, I just got back. Flew back last
22 night. It's beautiful there. Blue ocean. Redwoods. Food is
23 great. A lot of it organic. But I don't know Milt, those cats
24 out there are just a little too laid back, you know what I
25 mean? I couldn't take it. Mission District's got a little edge
26 to it. I had some fun there hanging out with some cool
27 dudes.
28   Yeah ... San Fran was very cool in the beginning but
29 then after a couple of weeks, I thought I would go crazy, so

1 I'm back. It was nice to get away. You just don't appreciate
2 New York until you get away from it. It's inside you ...
3 something about the beat of the city. Oh, there's Cup Crusher.
4 You know I missed him. Hey, there's some new cats falling for
5 Cup Crusher's schtick. Putting out the crumbs next to the
6 empty cups. Let's wait it out, let the new guys get a few pecks
7 from the crumbs and then we'll get the rest. In San Francisco
8 you mostly get whole wheat crumbs.
9   Oh man, look at that. There he goes, stomping on all the
10 cups. Oh wow! *(Looking up as the birds fly off.)* There they go,
11 those poor cats ... Heh heh, they'll be back later. Any new
12 cute birds around Milt? Hey, let's go get them crumbs. *(Back*
13 *to her standing self.)* Oh, here comes your bus. I got to be
14 moving on anyhow. I got places to go, people to see, things to
15 do. I got my 'to do' list right here in my pocket. You have a
16 nice night. It's a little cold tonight ain't it? I got gloves ...
17 just don't want to put them on yet. Say, uh, can you spare
18 some ... change? *(Pause.)* Oh, that's okay. I understand. No.
19 No. No. It's really alright. Hey lady, believe me, if anyone
20 understands, it's me. It's really okay. You have a nice night
21 and stay warm. What? *(Reaches out.)* Oh, thank you. *(Looks at*
22 *single coin her hand.)* Wow, I remember when you used to be
23 able to make a phone call with one of those. But that was a
24 long time ago. A long time ago. *(Pause.)*
25   *(WOMAN sees new person approaching the bus stop.)* You just
26 missed the bus, but there will be another one soon. See that
27 building? That is the ugliest building I ever seen. Man-oh-Man,
28 I never seen such an ugly building. That building is so ugly I
29 gotta get me a drink just to look at it. *(Takes drink.)*
30
31
32
33
34
35

Tough Cookies
by Edward Crosby Wells

1 Leota Ruth	Teen/Young Adult

2

3 *Leota Ruth, a young woman with a haunted look about her,*
4 *slowly enters her mother's kitchen carrying a bouquet of wild*
5 *flowers. There is something fragile and haunting in her lean and*
6 *gaunt appearance, almost like a frightened animal always on the*
7 *lookout for some unseen, silent predator. Leota Ruth's speech is*
8 *slow and deliberate, and she is constantly searching for some*
9 *deeper meaning in all she sees and hears.*

10

11 *(Announces.)* **Getting warm out there.** *(Looks for*
12 *confirmation. None comes. After a pause.)* **Morning ... And how**
13 **are you today?** *(Finding a tall water glass for the flowers. After*
14 *a pause.)* **And I am fine, too, thank you.** *(Arranging flowers in*
15 *glass.)* **Do you think flowers feel? Do they scream with pain**
16 **as you gather them up into a bouquet?** *(She looks about the*
17 *room for an answer. There is only silence.)* **No. I suppose not.**
18 **How could they? They are too beautiful. Beautiful things do**
19 **not feel.** *(After a pause.)* **Others feel for them. Do you think?**
20 **Filthy? They are not filthy, mother. Honest. I shook**
21 **them really well. I will put them in my room where they**
22 **cannot bother you. How sad. Weeds? You can only grow a**
23 **weed in a garden, mother. In the desert there are only**
24 **flowers — free and wild. My shoes. They seem to have come**
25 **untied.** *(While holding the glass of flowers, she puts her foot on*
26 *the chair.)* **Would you mind? My hands are full at the**
27 **moment. Thank you. Thank you so much.** *(Switches feet.)*
28 **This one, too, I'm afraid.**
29 **Sometimes, mother worries needlessly. I mean, I know**

1   how to tie my own shoes, of course. But, sometimes, when
2   your hands are full, you need a little help from others. Do you
3   think? I worry so, too. I worry that I will trip over my own laces
4   one day, step outside of time and space, and life will stroll on
5   down that endless and tedious road without me — forgetting I
6   was ever here. Where does it all go, those little variations in
7   time and space we call our lives?
8   *(To the open air. To no one in particular.)* **Sometimes there are**
9   **dueling voices in my mind ... rattling swords ... screaming for**
10 **attention. Noise. There is a mirror up ahead. I think I ought to**
11 **be reflected in it. But, the noise of those voices gets in the**
12 **way and keeps me from seeing where I am ... who I am. I**
13 **cannot see myself clearly. There is too much noise ... just too**
14 **much noise.** *(To audience.)* **The funny thing about my particular**
15 **kind of illness is that during those times of sanity ... the**
16 **inflicted person wants, more than anything, to be once again**
17 **engulfed in the illusions of the disease. It is a rare and ironic**
18 **comfort to the tormented party. To be sane in a sane world is**
19 **difficult enough, but to be sane in an insane world — well,**
20 **there's the rub.**
21
22
23
24
25
26
27
28
29
30
31
32
33
34
35

Downsizing
by Joseph Robinette

1   Samantha   Young Adult
2
3   *Samantha, a young woman in her mid-twenties, is serious and*
4   *has a clear sense of direction. Her spontaneous spirit of good fun*
5   *and humor signals an independent young lady with strong*
6   *personal values. Samantha has just learned that her company is*
7   *downsizing and new cost-cutting measures have been*
8   *announced. Armed with a small potted ficus plant, Samantha*
9   *offers her observations on the situation.*
10
11   Hello ... Say 'hi' to my ficus. You might know it better as
12   a rubber plant. I picked it up where I work. It's just been
13   fired. That's right — fired. And it had only been with the
14   corporation for about a month. That's why it's not very big.
15   Too young to get the axe, wouldn't you say? But, hey, that's
16   life in big corporate America — in the biggest *city* in
17   America. In fact all the plants got fired — the palms, the
18   ferns, the philodendrons. Newcomers and veterans alike. It
19   was a blood-letting. Or maybe I should say ... a chlorophyll-
20   letting. *(Taking out a half-sheet of folded paper.)*
21   We got this memo day before yesterday. *(Reading.)*
22   'McHugh Industries Incorporated, is hereby terminating its
23   forty-thousand-dollar-a-year plant watering contract in its
24   continuing efforts to reduce overhead during the current
25   economic slowdown. Employees are urged to take one or
26   more potted plants home. Those not taken will be thrown
27   away. This memo applies to both the Manhattan and New
28   England offices.'
29   *(To the audience.)* New England. I guess it's goodbye to

1 the *Boston* Ferns as well. Sorry — a little cost-cutting humor
2 there. Anyway, I decided to take *this* little guy ... or gal. How
3 do you tell the sex of a plant? *(A comic side.)* Look under their
4 leaves, dummy — ba-da-boom! *(Again to the audience.)* I only
5 took this *one.* My apartment in Brooklyn is very small. And
6 who knows how long I'll have it. When the plants go, can the
7 employees be far behind? Especially the junior staffers. You
8 know — last hired, first fired. But I can't even think about
9 going back home. I mean *home* home. Sparta, Illinois. Oh, it
10 was a nice place to grow up in — small, friendly. But once
11 you've been to Gotham, there's no turning back. I'm sure I can
12 find something here. I hope. I know they're always looking for
13 narrators on the Gray Line tours. It can't hurt that I majored
14 in communications at Southern Illinois University. And I heard
15 Zabar's is looking for a produce person. I worked at a farm
16 market for three summers in Sparta. It's a very fertile area.
17 Soil as black as ... New York sidewalks.
18   *(To the ficus.)* Come on, little ficus. We may be leaving
19 McHugh Industries, but we'll never depart the Big Apple.
20 Besides, you'd have a lot of competition in Sparta.
21 *Everybody's* got a potted plant there. Did I mention the place
22 is very fertile?
23
24
25
26
27
28
29
30
31
32
33
34
35

Othello Undercover
by Dave Tucker

1 Chelsea   Teen/Young Adult

2

3 *Chelsea, an egocentric young actress, attempts to make a*
4 *purchase at Computer Land, but is being ridiculed by an*
5 *unpleasant, unhelpful male sales clerk. The theatrical Chelsea*
6 *bravely plays the role of the captive classical heroine, and learns*
7 *to appreciate the joy and meaning of the computer world. She*
8 *refuses, however, to surrender her sense of pride in this computer*
9 *store confrontation.*

10

11   Okay, I'm losing my patience. I don't think I'm asking
12 too much. Now could you please tell me if you have one in
13 stock? Okay, for the last time, I need a ... DataMax CFS-
14 9000 Combination Digital Scanner-Photocopier-Facsimile
15 Machine. 'What am I going to use it for?' Who cares? What
16 difference does it make? The fact is, you little transistor-
17 headed geek — it's not even for me. I'm tracking it down for
18 a friend of mine who wants to get it as a gift for his wife,
19 and what happens to it after it leaves your store, is none of
20 your business ... So, you have one? Are you sure? Does it
21 have a USB connection? Does it have 4800 dpi? ... Are you
22 sure? No, I don't know what a dpi is — I just know that I
23 need 4800 of them ...
24   Don't get smart with me, you little jerk. Oh, you keep
25 that up and I'll reach over there and slap your pimply little
26 face ... You think that's funny? I'll tell you what's funny. Have
27 you ever been on a date? No, you haven't, have you? Now
28 that's funny! You know what else is funny? Let me guess.
29 You still live with your parents, you have a gargantuan comic

1   book collection and you've memorized the screenplays to all
2   the Star Trek movies. And what's more, you've never even
3   kissed a girl. Am I right? Oh ... hold on. I'm sorry. No, please,
4   no. Don't cry ... No, I didn't really mean it ... I'm just a little
5   upset. No, I'm sorry. I was just guessing ... No, I wouldn't say
6   that's pathetic ... Look, it's okay.
7   Now do you have one? Okay, that's great. Okay, thanks so
8   much. You're a real sweetheart. Thank you ... Thank you.
9   *(Under her breath.)* They just don't make men like they used to.
10
11
12
13
14
15
16
17
18
19
20
21
22
23
24
25
26
27
28
29
30
31
32
33
34
35

Lemonade Lagoon
by Christine Rusch

1   Marigold   Adult
2
3   *Marigold, a brassy mature woman, is pleased with her "good*
4   *catch," Cliff. Now, she is being formally introduced to her new in-*
5   *laws. Her speech is filled with colorful language and the in-laws*
6   *are spellbound with Marigold's antics. The true confessions*
7   *provided here only add to the hilarity of this larger-than-life social*
8   *misfit, who plays her role with gusto!*
9
10 My sister, she's got an acid stomach just like Cliff,
11 'cause she worries like him. *(LLOYD pours the Scotch.)* **Like**
12 **when we was takin' pictures, she goes 'Ain't you gonna get**
13 **a picture of Maureen?' And I says, 'No way ... I mean,**
14 **weddings are so kissy.' You go to a wedding and**
15 **everybody's kissin' everybody else. And when it's your**
16 **wedding, it's worse. Everybody's comin' up and kissin' you,**
17 **slobberin' all over you. But I ain't complainin'. I wouldn't**
18 **mind doin' it again sometime. Yeah, I got maybe three or**
19 **four real good kisses this morning, and then I see my**
20 **brother-in-law hangin' back there, and I go, 'C'mon, I can**
21 **use all the kissin' I can get!' So he gives me one, and Cliff**
22 **is standin' right there next to us, and he don't say a word.**
23 *(To CLIFF)* **What'dya think when you seen me walkin' up**
24 **there to you?** *(An awkward silence.)* **Know what I was**
25 **wearin'? White tulle. That's what it was made of. You bet**
26 **your bingo it was beautiful. Cowabunga, I was so all hanging**
27 **out gorgeous. Just like I am now. Ha, ha, ha. Bobby Harper**
28 **give me away. He goes, 'If you wasn't gettin' married today,**
29 **I'd marry you myself.' Ain't that sweet? Shoulda seen my**

1   brother. He comes up before the ceremony, and he goes,
2   'Everyone looks so nice. I don't wanna go in a church lookin'
3   like this,' and I go, 'Shut up.' Yeah, it's better than elopin'. I
4   done that the first couple of times, and I'm tellin' you, you get
5   more stuff this way. Plus with the pre-nup I get to keep my
6   wedding gifts, no matter what.
7   I mean, we got silver and china, and all that stuff. And you
8   wouldn't believe the food. Cripes, by the end of it all, I felt like
9   a stuffed pig. I mean, they wouldn't believe how much food we
10 had. We had enough to open our own grocery. Bet you think I
11 tossed my bouquet? Naw. Gave it to Carlton for Ginger's
12 wedding. Poor Carlton. He's this guy I usta date. His step-
13 daughter, her name is Ginger, and you know what? She's
14 gettin' married tomorrow. I mean, can you believe it? Only one
15 day earlier and her and me woulda had the same weddin'
16 anniversary ... 'Course, he pretty near forgot it, 'cause the
17 thing about Carlton was he always did party long and hard.
18 Come to think of it, I don't know if he took them flowers or not,
19 being as after the band left I seen him over on the floor near
20 the bandstand, just layin' there, so I went over to him, and he
21 was out cold. I was afraid they was going to have to give him
22 artificial insemination. *(She helps herself to another beer.)*
23
24
25
26
27
28
29
30
31
32
33
34
35

The Food Monologues
by Kerri Kochanski

1   Suzanne   Young Adult

2

3   *Suzanne, an anxious, thin young woman, sits cross-legged in the*
4   *center of the floor surrounded by an assortment of food. Her lips*
5   *smeared with mustard, Suzanne hungrily eyes the Girl Scout*
6   *cookies, wedding cake topper, and other foods that are easily*
7   *within her reach. She holds one hand behind her back, feeling*
8   *guilty that her husband has discovered her haunting secret.*

9

10   You look stumped like ... you don't know what's going
11 on — and I don't either. I mean if I did I would *tell* you ... I
12 mean why this crab is in my pocket ... *(She takes a cooked*
13 *crab out of her pocket.)* Why I have mustard on my lips ... and
14 cookies ... Let's not forget about the cookies. *(Reminding*
15 *him.)* The cookies that were *sitting* there in the *back* of the
16 closet for *ten months* ... *Ten months*, Angelo. And when I
17 was looking for my coat I saw ... Saw because ... I don't
18 know — I *wanted* to see. It was *time* to see. Time to see
19 that by hiding the cookies in the closet ... By hiding the
20 crabs and the cakes ... *(He doesn't understand. She reiterates.)*
21   Cake ... *(She takes a large piece of wedding cake from*
22 *behind her back.)* Yes, cake ... And it's not because it's our
23 anniversary. It's because it's *cake* and I'm *hungry!* *(She*
24 *waits as he responds. Arguing.)* I don't *care* if the cake topper
25 is lonely ... I want to eat it ... And cookies and crabs ... And
26 whatever else you've got hidden away in there — in the back
27 of the closet, in the back of the refrigerator. It's my
28 refrigerator, too. I should get to *see* to *see* things ... *(She*
29 *remembers.)*

1   The wedding's over ... *(Beat.)* **So I really don't have to be**
2   **skinny anymore. You know I really don't need to be skinny ...**
3   *(She doesn't know what to do. Notices the crab.)* **Crabs won't**
4   **make me fat ...** *(She picks up the crab. Begins to internalize.)* **But**
5   **they'll be there. Be my friend ... When I don't have a friend.**
6   *(Firmly, regurgitating.)* **Because** *cake* **is no friend.** *Cookies* ...
7   *(Strongly.)* **They are** *food,* **Angelo. They are** *food* ... *(She begins*
8   *to get agitated, dependent.)* **And I** *want* **them ... I** *need* **them ...**
9   *(Momentously.)* **I** *found* **them ...** *(She remembers.)* **Found them ...**
10 *(Vulnerable.)* **Before I found you.**
11
12
13
14
15
16
17
18
19
20
21
22
23
24
25
26
27
28
29
30
31
32
33
34
35

Curse of the Devil
by Kent R. Brown

1 Melissa   Teen/Young Adult

2

3 *Melissa, a country girl in her late teens, comes from a long line of*
4 *vision healers. She is a free spirit with considerable charm and*
5 *unfailing warmth, but is also pregnant. Melissa is testifying before*
6 *an assembly of believers, unburdening herself as she comes to*
7 *terms with her awesome talent. There is also an emotional struggle*
8 *taking place here as she tries to reconcile her vision with reality.*

9

10 We was livin' in Mississippi, me and Mama, my
11 Grandma Jenny and Grandpa Ezekiel. Grandpa Ezekiel was
12 dyin' and each day at sunset ... Grandma Jenny would open
13 her hands, hold 'em over Grandpa Ezekiel's back and slowly
14 lower them onto his skin ... and press her fingers into his
15 muscles ... all knotted up from the effort of dyin'. And she'd
16 touch his back and soothe his achin' body. And she'd touch
17 his scars, too. And with each touch she had a vision ... a
18 vision of what thing had caused the scar. That time when
19 Grandpa Ezekiel was seven years old, out in the field, hot
20 'n' dusty, and he fell and hurt his knee and started cryin'
21 and Great Grandpa reached high in the air with his
22 horsewhip. 'You ain't no little girl, boy. You get up now!
23 Time to plow the field!' And Great Grandpa's whip came
24 down hard on Grandpa Ezekiel's back ... again and again.
25 Grandma Jenny could feel the whip cuttin' through her
26 fingers as she touched his back. They felt on fire.
27   When my Mama turned thirteen, Grandma Jenny called
28 her inside the house. She shut all the windows and doors.
29 Then she took off Mama's clothes and then Grandma Jenny

1   took her own clothes off 'n' they was standin' face to face.
2   Then Grandma Jenny took Mama's hands and placed them on
3   Grandma Jenny's naked body, on her neck, her breasts, her
4   legs. 'Tell me, darlin', what you see. You tell me now.' And
5   Mama began to see! And to feel! 'Oh, please, Mama, don't
6   make me see.' But she did ... that time one Sunday afternoon
7   when Grandma Jenny was raped by the Freeman brothers the
8   summer they was workin' Grandpa Ezekiel's farm when he
9   was sick with influenza. *(Beat.)* After the vision my Mama and
10   Grandma Jenny held each other close and felt the shame of
11   the past.
12   After Grandma Jenny died, people came up to the door and
13   asked Mama if she'd come down to Sherman Junction and
14   touch the afflicted. And she did. She'd place her hands on their
15   legs and arms, stomachs ... backs curved with pain. And she
16   saw it all ... felt it all. Their fears, doubts, the pain of broken
17   hearts ... the pain that hatreds bring. And they all felt better.
18   Mama took their pain away. *(Beat.)* But at the end of the day
19   she'd shut her bedroom door. Then I heard the screams and I'd
20   peek into her room. She'd be thrashin' on her bed ... and all the
21   voices of the people she'd touched that day screamin' out of her
22   mouth — the beggin', the anger, the lamentations.
23   People said that Mama had the sweetest touch in the
24   world. But each time she got more and more tired, went to
25   bed for three whole days ... sometimes more. She tried to stop
26   touchin' people but she couldn't. One mornin' she called me
27   to her bedside. 'Your Grandma Jenny had the touch. And I
28   have the touch. And you will, too.' And she took my hand and
29   pressed it to her heart. 'It's a gift from God, child, and a curse
30   from the Devil. Now, you can keep to yourself ... or you can
31   heal the wounds of others. But that pain's gotta go
32   somewhere, child. And one day you'll pay the price.'
33   I ain't touched nobody yet, not even to shake their hands.
34   And when me and Matthew Silas went down by the river and
35   made a baby, I held two rocks in my hands so I wouldn't hold

1   him close. He didn't seem to mind. I'm gonna be a mama
2   soon. I know it's a girl 'cause when I touch my belly I can see
3   her. But I shouldn't touch no one 'til I have the baby. 'Fraid
4   the sins and the screams of other people will hide inside her
5   heart. But every day I get an urge ... it pushes me ... stronger
6   'n' stronger. I'll touch someone some day, I know I will 'n'
7   that'll mean my child will have the curse of the Devil, too. Just
8   like me. *(Extending her arms to the audience.)* **Let me touch your**
9   **faces ... just once. I can take away your pain ... please?**
10
11
12
13
14
15
16
17
18
19
20
21
22
23
24
25
26
27
28
29
30
31
32
33
34
35

Cherchez Dave Robicheaux
by Nina Lanai Wright

1 Britteney   Young Adult/Adult
2
3 *Britteney, an attractive and vain former beauty queen, is now*
4 *hosting a local A.M. television show, "Good Morning, Goshen!"*
5 *She is usually elegant and sophisticated, but as she anxiously*
6 *stands in front of the camera Britteney appears to be very*
7 *distracted. She spends most of her air time trying to explain her*
8 *disheveled appearance, even as she breaks the biggest news story*
9 *of her career!*
10
11   Good morning, Goshen! I think you can plainly see that
12 what we have here is an Emergency Broadcast Situation.
13 No, the good old U.S. of A.'s not under attack — I think
14 we'd be playing sirens or something if that was happening —
15 but it might as well be for all the trauma Yours Truly
16 endured last night in the service of her viewing public. *(She*
17 *rises and soberly approaches the camera.)*
18   At approximately five — o — nine p.m., I was called
19 upon to cover the stunning arrest of kidnapper and serial
20 killer Elizabeth Bye Harkness — across from the Bowl 'n'
21 Brew in Elkhart. What ensued can only be described as the
22 biggest bungle in E.P.D. history. That's right, folks, she got
23 away! And — shades of Patty Hearst — whoever that is,
24 somebody my middle-aged boss told me to mention — the
25 kidnapper's victim has joined the Other Side! Yes, Mrs.
26 Norma Rhinderknecht was last seen fleeing the Elkhart
27 Mini-Mall with her abductor!
28   And now — my Exclusive Report: 'Bungle Near the Bowl
29 'n' Brew: How the Elkhart P.D. Blew It.'

1   First, permit me to say a few words about my appearance
2 this morning. See, here at Channel 6, if you're Talent — that's
3 me — you don't get the services of a full-time professional hair
4 and make-up artist. Can you believe it? Incredible but true.
5 The reason why I look so good ninety — nine — point — nine
6 percent of the time is because I know hair and make-up.
7 Obviously. But last night, while I was on special high-risk field
8 assignment, I was personally attacked. That's right. What
9 happened   next   was   an   unfortunate   series   of
10 misunderstandings between me and the E.P.D. To make a long
11 story short, Yours Truly was forced to spend the night in a
12 holding cell. Thank goodness the only other people in that ...
13 room ... were two passed-out drunks and a harmless,
14 babbling street person named Delilah.
15   As for what went wrong at the scene, I can only say that I
16 was apparently duped by the serial murderer's accomplice,
17 who claimed to be Cher's road manager. A natural mistake on
18 my part. He promised me an exclusive interview with the
19 Super Diva herself, provided I waited for her behind the
20 dumpster. That seemed a reasonable request. But while I was
21 waiting, amid the flies and the stench, along came the killer,
22 who told me her name was Electra Rockaway. Being the Ace
23 reporter that I am, I immediately recognized her as Elizabeth
24 Bye Harkness, Fugitive from Justice, and tried to signal a
25 police officer. But there was none in the vicinity. I later learned
26 that they were all trying to get Cher's autograph.
27   Ladies and Gentlemen — I now have reason to believe that
28 Cher was never in Elkhart last night! That's right. Anyhow ...
29 Elizabeth Bye Harkness, alias Electra Rockaway, is a cunning
30 criminal. Before I knew what hit me that little tramp, I mean,
31 vixen, bit me on the arm, momentarily immobilizing me. And
32 then she summoned the police by screaming that she had
33 cornered a notorious drug pusher. Can you believe that?
34   As many of you no doubt recall, I competed for the title of
35 Miss Indiana 1998 on a Drug Free Schools platform. You may

1   remember my slogan, 'Say no to narcotics!' Well, Elkhart's
2   Finest must have missed the pageant. They arrested me and
3   allowed a known felon to flee into the night. I know what
4   you're thinking — about the unspeakable — stuff that could
5   have happened to a girl like me. But I'm all right. Only a few
6   short minutes before we went on the air this morning I was
7   finally sprung from the slammer by my boss and producer ...
8   who shall remain nameless. Read the credits!
9
10
11
12
13
14
15
16
17
18
19
20
21
22
23
24
25
26
27
28
29
30
31
32
33
34
35

Kitchen Sink Drama
by Andrew Biss

1 Joy   Adult

2

3 *Joy, an independent and self-absorbed woman on the go, has*
4 *just arrived late at the home of her sister, Elaine. Joy doesn't*
5 *appear to be anxious or expectant after receiving a distressing*
6 *message from her sister earlier in the day. In typical fashion,*
7 *Joy's entrance is swift, brash, and bombastic. She is oblivious to*
8 *the events of the moment and is unable to comprehend the*
9 *seriousness of her sister's message.*

10

11   Darling, my apologies, you must forgive me, but it's
12 Wednesday, as you know — the day I have to take
13 Stephen's brats to the park. Hideous, I know, but what can
14 you do? And so there I am, sitting on this hideously
15 uncomfortable wooden bench that's covered in lichen and
16 bird excrement, being subjected to the most appalling high-
17 pitched squeals and laughter emanating from those pre-
18 pubescent monsters from Stephen's squalid little pre-me
19 marriage, wondering what on earth I'd done to deserve it all,
20 when I attempt — in desperation — to make contact with
21 the outside world and check my messages, and wouldn't
22 you know it ... the lousy phone's out of juice. So, then I
23 have to drag these two creatures, kicking and screaming
24 needless to say, to the nearest wine bar where I can plug in
25 and recharge — me and the bloody phone — them crying
26 and sobbing the whole three hours, of course — even
27 though I'd bought them more magazines and fizzy drinks
28 than you could possibly imagine — until I finally get a
29 signal, got your hideous message, unloaded the brats back

1   onto Stephen and charged over here as if my life depended on
2   it. So how are you, darling? Well, obviously you're feeling
3   completely hideous — but, I mean, other than that?
4   Everything all right?

5

6

7

8

9

10

11

12

13

14

15

16

17

18

19

20

21

22

23

24

25

26

27

28

29

30

31

32

33

34

35

An American Daughter
by Wendy Wasserstein

1   Dr. Judith B. Kaufman   Adult
2
3   *Judith, an African-American and Jewish oncologist, is the best*
4   *friend of Lyssa Dent Hughes, controversial nominee for a*
5   *congressional appointment whose confirmation unravels because*
6   *she threw away a jury duty notice. Judith offers her*
7   *unconditional support to Lyssa and provides some sharp comic*
8   *political commentary in the colorful retelling of her own*
9   *"drowning" incident in the Potomac River!*
10
11   I went to the Festival of Regrets. I prayed by the banks
12 of the Potomac. There were old men davening in prayer
13 shawls, and young lawyers in Brooks Brothers suits. I
14 watched while the men tossed in their breadcrumbs of
15 secret sorrow. 'Oh, Lord, my God, I cheated on my income
16 tax.' 'Oh, Lord of the universe, I lust for the Asian checkout
17 girl at Hany Farms delicatessen.' 'Oh, Lord, I have sinned,
18 I dreamt about a strip of bacon.' At first I remained silent.
19 I stood there feeling my familiar distance and disdain. And
20 then, almost involuntarily, I began shredding my low-fat
21 cranberry-orange muffin. I wanted this God, this Yaveh, to
22 know me.
23   So I tossed my first crumb into the water. 'Oh, Lord, my
24 God, King of the universe, I have failed to honor my mother
25 and father,' and that regret floats out to Maryland. 'Oh,
26 Lord, my God, I distrust most people I know, I feel no
27 comfort in their happiness, no sympathy for their sorrow.' A
28 tiny cranberry sits still upon the water. 'Oh, Lord, our God,
29 who is like you in Earth or in Heaven, I regret the men I've

1   been with, I regret the marriage I made, I regret never having
2   children, I regret never having learned to be a woman.' I pull
3   off the entire top and a wad of muffin sails like a frigate
4   towards the Washington Monument. 'Oh, Lord, my God,
5   Mighty of Mighty, Holy of Holy, I can't make life and I can't
6   stop death. Oh, Lord, my God, the Lord is one, I've wasted my
7   life,' and I jump in.
8   I was bobbing up and down in my pearls and Liz Claiborne
9   suit, when I noticed a box of Dunkin' Donut holes floating
10 along. And suddenly I remembered the slogan from my
11 mother's favorite donut shop, 'As you ramble on through life,
12 whatever be your goal, keep your eye upon the donut, and not
13 upon the hole.' And I began laughing and laughing. Now I had
14 a purpose. Now I had a goal. I must rescue the donut holes
15 and bring them here to you on N Street. Lyssa, these are the
16 donut holes of my discontent!
17
18
19
20
21
22
23
24
25
26
27
28
29
30
31
32
33
34
35

The Sphere Hunt
by Nancy Gall-Clayton

1   Irene   Adult

2

3   *A politically correct, middle school teacher encourages spellbound*
4   *volunteers to become active participants in an after-school "sphere*
5   *hunt." The tongue-in-cheek character sketch is filled with colorful*
6   *language and flavorful tidbits of innuendo that should be a crowd-*
7   *pleaser! The "peacemaker" teacher offers a whimsical excursion*
8   *into the world of parenting and middle school education.*

9

10   Thank you for volunteering! Our After-School Sphere
11 Hunt promises to be fabulous — although I'm afraid there's
12 been a slight misunderstanding. Gentleman in the back row
13 with the spears — *(Clears throat.)* — it's a hunt for *spheres.*
14   We were going to call it an Oval Hunt, but even in middle
15 school, the kids know an oval is two-dimensional. We
16 decided against Holiday Hunt because that name would
17 suggest that our event was inspired by a holiday, and the
18 next thing you know we'd be offending Seventh Day
19 Adventists, Jews, Hindus, Buddhists, Wicca, and the ACLU.
20 We thought of Ov*um* Hunt, which is 100% accurate and
21 simultaneously teaches a bit of Latin, but Right-to-Life
22 might have objected to 'ovum' and made us call it a Chick
23 Hunt. *(Clears throat.)* How many parents would let their
24 children stay after school to hunt chicks — of either variety?
25   So Sphere Hunt it is, no weapons required, but because
26 so many children are tall and obese these days and so many
27 of you have had face lifts, we're providing Elliptical Ears to
28 each of you. Wear them at all times so you can quickly be
29 identified as an adult volunteer. At first glance, they may

1   look like — *(Hushed tone for next two words.)* — bunny ears, but
2   please don't refer to them that way. It will only confuse the
3   children.
4   One final note: This is a fun fest, not a competition. As the
5   mission statement of this school so eloquently explains,
6   competition — or more accurately, losing — can damage
7   egos. Therefore, all spheres will be deposited in a centrally
8   located Sphere Pile. Direct each child in your group to the
9   Sphere Pile as soon as he or she locates one. Discourage
10 them from tallying of any kind. It doesn't matter who finds the
11 most. Or the least.
12   At the end of the event, we will divide the number of
13 children by the number of spheres in the pile, and with your
14 able assistance, each child will arrive at his or her respective
15 home with exactly the same number of spheres as every other
16 child. Elliptical ears are on the table up front. Are there any
17 questions?
18
19
20
21
22
23
24
25
26
27
28
29
30
31
32
33
34
35

The Apostle John
by Jeff Goode

1	Nikki and Mary	Teens/Young Adults
2		

3   *Duolog*

4   *Sometimes poignant and sometimes provocative, this duolog*
5   *features two young women whose conflicting convictions on*
6   *the subject of religion and spiritual piety offer a sobering*
7   *glimpse of the potentially volatile nature of trying to impose*
8   *one's own beliefs and values on others. Although the theme*
9   *is serious, there is a comic sense of frivolity in both the dialog*
10   *and the action as the characters struggle to define their*
11   *individual and personal points of view. There is also an*
12   *interesting mixture of images in this duolog generally*
13   *associated with "absurdism" — the setting, for example, is a*
14   *public restroom — that might suggest a symbolic allegory or*
15   *parable is being told about present-day society. In playing the*
16   *scene some attention should be paid to movement and*
17   *staging that suggests the characters are solitary figures*
18   *isolated in time and space. Keep the character portraits*
19   *simple, rather than theatrical, to underscore the realistic*
20   *action being depicted. Remember to allow the laughable to*
21   *emerge as the result of character actions performed, rather*
22   *than as a conscious attempt to provoke humor.*

23

24   *Mary, a mysterious young woman with a piercing eye on*
25   *human nature, stands alone in a corner of a public restroom,*
26   *waiting contentedly. Enter, somewhat urgently, Nikki, a*
27   *naive but high-spirited woman with youthful exuberance.*
28   *Following a series of awkward and silent moments, Nikki*
29   *moves quickly from one locked stall to another and then*

1   *halts abruptly when she glimpses Mary.*

2   NIKKI: **Sorry!** *(She tries the door to the second stall. It is locked,*

3   *too.)* **Sorry!** *(NIKKI stands off to one side to wait. She looks*

4   *around, antsily. She notices MARY, smiling benevolently.)*

5   MARY: Hi.

6   NIKKI: Hi.

7   MARY: You got a minute?

8   NIKKI: What? Why?

9   MARY: Do you have a minute?

10 NIKKI: No! I mean, why? A minute for what? What do you need?

11 MARY: I just want to ask you something?

12 NIKKI: Oh. Sure, okay. Ask me what?

13 MARY: Have you accepted Jesus Christ as your personal savior?

14 NIKKI: Ah geez!

15 MARY: I guess that's a 'no,' huh?

16 NIKKI: *(Looking for a way out.)* Uh ...

17 MARY: Can I ask you something else?

18 NIKKI: Y'know, I'm in kind of a hurry. I really gotta go. I

19   mean, I gotta 'go,' and then I gotta get out of here. I'm

20   right in the middle of this thing.

21 MARY: Yeah, me, too ... It seems like we're always in the

22   middle of something, though, doesn't it? Lunch date, or

23   a meeting or a lunch meeting or a conference call. Middle

24   of work. Middle of school. Middle of life. No time. Not a

25   minute to spare ... No time for Jesus.

26 NIKKI: Yeah. Bummer. *(Long pause as they both look at each*

27   *other.)*

28 MARY: Did you hear that?

29 NIKKI: What? *(They both listen.)*

30 MARY: There it is again.

31 NIKKI: What? What?

32 MARY: That silence. That's the saddest sound in the world.

33   That's the sound of me not telling you about Jesus. And

34   you not having time to hear me if I did.

35 NIKKI: Look, I don't want to get into this right now.

1   MARY: Oh, me neither. That's the last thing I want to do. But
2   you really leave me no choice.
3   NIKKI: I leave you no choice?
4   MARY: You have to go to the bathroom, don't you?
5   NIKKI: What?
6   MARY: Do you know how many people die on the toilet each
7   year? More than you'd think. Trying too hard, I guess. It's
8   our competitive nature. Can't leave well enough alone.
9   Gotta fight. Gotta win. Gotta ... *(She gives a long*
10   *scatological grunt, then ...)* Bam! Pop an aneurysm and
11   you're gone like that.
12   NIKKI: That's disgusting.
13   MARY: You think that's bad? Try dying on a toilet and then
14   being cast into a lake of fire right after. That's really
15   gotta suck.
16   NIKKI: Okay, that's enough.
17   MARY: I don't know you. You don't know me. After this, we
18   may never see each other again.
19   NIKKI: Please, God, let that be true.
20   MARY: How do you think I'd feel if you went in there and
21   dropped dead and I just stood by and didn't even try to
22   throw you a life line?
23   NIKKI: Hey, I don't need a life line.
24   MARY: You don't need one? Oh, I see you've got it all figured
25   out. When the Judgment Day comes, you're just going to
26   walk right up to the Heavenly Father and say, 'Look at
27   my schedule! When did I have time for salvation?
28   Thursday I was in meetings all day, and Friday I had that
29   lunch, and you know how tired I am at the end of the day,
30   so let's not do it in the evening, and sure there was that
31   minute I had in the bathroom, but that's my alone time.
32   I need to focus. I can't have somebody looking out for my
33   eternal well-being.'
34   NIKKI: Okay, look, lady, this is neither the time, nor the place.
35   MARY: You're right. No problem. Why don't I catch you later

1   then?

2 NIKKI: Good idea.

3 MARY: How about the next time you're in church? When will

4   that be? This Sunday? Next Sunday? The week after that?

5 NIKKI: I don't go to church, if that's what you're getting at.

6 MARY: And you probably don't want me bugging you at the

7   airport either.

8 NIKKI: No, I don't want you bugging me anywhere.

9 MARY: So, it's not really the time or the place that bothers

10   you at all, is it?

11 NIKKI: Yes! Yes, it is! This is a public restroom, for Christ's

12   sake!

13 MARY: If only that were true. You know, they say that God is

14   everywhere. But I don't think He's here. I don't think He's

15   in a public restroom. You never hear stories about a good

16   bowel movement bringing a person closer to God. You

17   never see someone sitting in a stall with their head

18   bowed in prayer, thanking the Lord for the precious gift

19   of a clean urinary tract. God's blessings are all around

20   us, everywhere you look, except here. Here it's just you,

21   and me ... and temptation.

22 NIKKI: Now hold on!

23 MARY: You say this isn't the place for religion, but I say this

24   room needs it more than anywhere else on Earth.

25 NIKKI: *(Knocking on the stall door.)* Hurry up in there!

26 MARY: *(Going for the kill.)* You're like the Lord Jesus Christ,

27   knocking at the door to someone's heart, but she won't

28   let Him in. But what else can He do? He can't peek over

29   the top. That wouldn't be right. But no one's answering,

30   and He has to get in there. He can't slide under, can He?

31   But maybe that's what the Lord Jesus is doing right now.

32   Maybe He's sent me to slide under the door to the toilet

33   of your heart to save your soul with His holy touch.

34 NIKKI: *(Backing away.)* Don't you touch me.

35 MARY: What are you afraid of?

1 NIKKI: I'm afraid of you creeping me out is what! I'm afraid
2   this is a public restroom and I gotta take a pee and I'd
3   like some privacy, but you're getting in my personal
4   space and it's freaking me out!
5 MARY: No, I think what's really freaking you out is that you
6   don't have Christ Jesus in your personal space. And
7   without Him, you're just a lonely sinner cornered in a
8   dirty women's room by a dangerous psychotic who
9   believes in crazy fairy tales and won't leave you alone
10   until she makes you believe what she believes.
11 NIKKI: Yes! Yes, that's it!
12 MARY: But with Him, you're never alone and you're never in
13   danger because it's not crazy, because the fairy tales are
14   true, and all you have to do is let yourself believe them.
15 NIKKI: *(Pleading.)* Please, just leave me alone, I'm begging you.
16 MARY: Will you accept Jesus Christ as your personal Lord
17   and savior?
18 NIKKI: Yes, yes, I'll do whatever you want!
19 MARY: Will you let Him into your heart and into your soul?
20 NIKKI: Yes, anything, please! I just want to go to the bathroom.
21   *(MARY falls to her knees and 'joins' NIKKI in prayer.)*
22 MARY: Lord Jesus, hear this sinner's prayers. Fill her with
23   the Holy Spirit, and grant her relief from her worldly
24   suffering and a life everlasting with you in Paradise. We
25   ask it in your holy name. Amen. *(NIKKI is sobbing as MARY*
26   *finishes praying.)*
27 NIKKI: Oh God ... Oh God ... *(Then MARY crawls under the*
28   *door to the stall and opens it from the inside. The stall is*
29   *empty.)* What the — ? *(MARY gives the dumbfounded NIKKI*
30   *a hug and walks out, smiling contentedly.)*
31
32
33
34
35

Chapter VI

The Golden Age

I do not ask for any crown
But that which all may win;
Nor try to conquer any world
Except the one within.

— *Louisa May Alcott,* My Kingdom

Golden age monolog characters are mature, resolute stage figures whose life experiences and admirable values, principles, or morals set them apart from other characters. Their insights and observations offer a "memory book" of personal or unique stories that are faithfully direct and sensitive. These are characters of varying ages, physical dimensions, social status, emotional or intellectual capacity, and world view. They have performed acts of self-sacrifice, exhibited courage and cowardice sometimes simultaneously, engaged in ignorant blunders, or committed errors in judgment. They have also suffered in silence and are just now speaking out.

The one common theme each character brings to our understanding of the golden age is that they serve as witnesses to the surging tides of time, truth, and the human condition. The characters use simple thoughts to express complex emotions, and exhibit personal satisfaction in giving meaning to their life stories. They capture the universal flavor and spirit of the meaning of life and the nature of human despair and suffering. There are also poignant moments of confused bewilderment, comic insight, unpredictable outbursts, and slapstick humor that punctuate the riddles and mysteries voiced by these characters.

In playing the monologs your concern should be to appear sane and sensible no matter what the situation or the character behavior. Allow the true meaning of the actions and words of the characters to emerge in subtle gestures and facial expressions that mirror their interior feelings and thoughts. There should be a more mature attitude at work in developing these character portraits. Peer beneath the sometimes obvious or superficial exterior of the characters to discover the essential qualities that may provide imaginative approaches to performance. You will need a more three-dimensional character portrait that is believable and honest because it is based on a real-life role model that addresses universal themes and values.

Summer
by Edward Bond

1   Marthe   Adult
2
3   *Two mature women, who were respectively servant and mistress in*
4   *an occupied area of Europe during World War II, are reunited.*
5   *Marthe, the servant, is now dying of an incurable disease. The*
6   *mistress, Ann, who collaborated with the enemy to save her*
7   *servant's life, now visits Marthe in the old house they used to share.*
8   *Their reunion reopens past wounds, but also reveals eternal bonds.*
9
10 *(Working.)* **What's more useless than death? Life without**
11 **death would be. How could you find anything beautiful if you**
12 **looked at it forever? You'd grow tired of it. Why fall in love if**
13 **it lasted forever? When you'd forgiven yourselves a thousand**
14 **times you'd tire of forgiveness. You'd grow tired of changing**
15 **the people you loved.**
16 *(ANN returns with three folded chairs, opens them and sets*
17 *them at the table.)*
18   **If you ate for eternity why bother to taste what you're**
19 **eating? You can taste the next meal. When you've cried for**
20 **one mistake you wouldn't cry for the next. You'd have**
21 **eternity to put it right. Soon your eyes would be full of sleep.**
22 **You'd go deaf. You wouldn't listen to voices because they**
23 **would give you the trouble of answering. Why listen to**
24 **them? It would be useless to know which was a sparrow or**
25 **a waterfall. In eternity there would be no future. You'd sit on**
26 **the ground and turn to stone. Dust would pile up and bury**
27 **you. If we didn't die we'd live like the dead. Without death**
28 **there's no life. No beauty, love or happiness. You can't laugh**
29 **for more than a few hours or weep more than a few days. No**

1   one could bear more than our life. Only hell could be eternal.
2   Sometimes life is cruel and death is sudden — that's the price
3   we pay for not being stones. Don't let the lightning strike you
4   or madmen burn your house. Don't give yourself to your
5   enemies or neglect anyone in need. Fight. But in the end
6   death is a friend who brings a gift: life. Not for you but the
7   others. I die so that you might live. Did you call David?
8   Breakfast's ready.
9
10
11
12
13
14
15
16
17
18
19
20
21
22
23
24
25
26
27
28
29
30
31
32
33
34
35

Relationships
by Ken Friedman

1 Bookworm   Young Adult/Adult
2
3 *The Bookworm, a young woman, is desperate for advice on*
4 *pursuing successful relationships. She has purchased a do-it-*
5 *yourself textbook titled* Relationships for Romantic Wrecks *and*
6 *is now reading it aloud to her friends. Although there is an*
7 *underlying tone of anguish in the Bookworm's romantic notions,*
8 *she slowly realizes that she is a complete person and not just an*
9 *occasional date.*
10
11   Okay, I'm ready now. This girl is prepared! I have the
12 book. *Relationships for Romantic Wrecks.* A best-seller.
13 From now on, my love life is guaranteed. Chapter One: First
14 date. 'Don't be obscene, silly, stupid, negative or whiney.'
15 Wow, what insights! What's the next nugget: 'Don't spit in
16 your soup'? Oh, let me go on. I can't wait to share. 'Say
17 something nice to him.' Oh, my God! Why didn't I think of
18 that? Another major breakthrough! 'Compliment his hair.'
19 Okay. How about, 'I love your hair. Who needs more than
20 one?' 'But, if he's bald, make another choice.' Okay, here
21 goes: 'Golly, Jeff, you have beautiful teeth. Gray is my
22 favorite color.' 20 dollars. I spent 20 dollars, but I say it's
23 worth every penny. Let me give you a whiff of Chapter Two.
24 'Never have sex with anyone until you know their middle
25 name.' So, that's what I've been doing wrong! You have to
26 know the middle name, and for all these years I've been
27 happy with a first initial. But, what if he doesn't have a
28 middle name? Then what? Are we doomed to celibacy? And,
29 if on the first date, he should ask for mine, do I slap the pig

1   in the face? 'My middle name? Sir, what kind of a girl do you
2   think I am?'
3   Wham! 20 dollars and bought by both men and women
4   and me! I bought it! Why? What level have I sunk to that I have
5   so little confidence in my own intelligence that I need to read
6   a book that tells me how to behave? I have met many men. I
7   have had many relationships. I have been rejected. I have
8   been lied to. I have been used and insulted. Oh yes, just like
9   you! And I have been rude on many occasions and frightened,
10   just like us all. Who survives unscathed? We all butcher the
11   innocent. Oh, I've made my share of big mistakes and
12   committed numerous sad and poor behaviors. I regret so
13   much, but I regret nothing more than having reached the point
14   where I bought this book — until I realized that it's a
15   wonderful book, because it reminded me that I don't need it.
16   Do you hear me? I still have pride, intelligence, and some
17   character and I am a person first and a date second. I am a
18   woman and an adult and I can think for myself and you can
19   take this book, my friends, and ... on the other hand, nobody
20   forced me to buy it. No one held a gun to my head. So why did
21   I buy it, if I didn't need it? Why? How frightened am I? Just
22   how frightened have I become? So, who here wants to read a
23   book? Anyone?
24
25
26
27
28
29
30
31
32
33
34
35

Dead Man's Handle
by John Constable

1 Woman   Adult
2
3 *A woman of unspecified age stands quietly beside the bed of a man*
4 *on a life-support machine in a British hospital. The woman is in*
5 *shock as she gazes at the monitors and the tubes that are attached*
6 *to the listless man. The woman sits and struggles to cope with her*
7 *fears. Though grieving, she valiantly expresses her thoughts to the*
8 *man and we gradually learn more about their relationship.*
9
10   **Sorry I'm late. Took me forever to get here. Incident on**
11 **the Piccadilly Line ... You won't believe this — they had a**
12 **runaway tube train! Driver gets out to check the door. Train**
13 **pulls out, rattles on through the next station. So then, of**
14 **course, the whole system grinds to a halt while they check**
15 **the line. We were stuck in the tunnel for over an hour. By**
16 **the time we got out it was in the late edition.** *(She opens her*
17 *evening paper, scanning the report, as if keeping up to date with*
18 *the news.)*
19   **Apparently it's technically possible for trains to move**
20 **without the driver — although the brakes are supposed to**
21 **engage automatically if the driver's handle — it's funny,**
22 **they call it the 'dead man's handle' ... is ... released.** *(Her*
23 *voice trails off. She throws down the paper, gets up and lights a*
24 *cigarette, pacing around the bed, distractedly taking several drags*
25 *before she realizes she's smoking in a hospital.)*
26   **Oh God — what am I doing?** *(She stamps out the*
27 *cigarette.)* **Be just like me to go and set off the alarm.** *(She*
28 *sits back down, staring at the man. Pause.)* **Hello ... It's me.**
29 **Remember? Are you there? Hello? Anyone there? You**

1   always think somehow there'll be ... time ... to say the things
2   you ... And then it's too late ... No one to hear it ... *(Pause.)*
3   Listen! I don't want to lose you. But, to see you like this ...
4   reduced to ... I know. It's selfish ... I say to myself 'For *your*
5   sake. I don't want you to suffer' — but what I mean is, 'I don't
6   want to *see* you suffer.' I just ... can't bear this ... dead weight
7   of seeing someone I love slowly wasting away before my eyes.
8   I want to close my eyes and picture you as I knew you, with
9   all your faculties intact. But this ... This isn't you. Is it? If they
10   could heal you, somehow ... restore you, make you whole
11   again ... But if they can't, I wish ... I wish they'd just let
12   you ... *(Pause. She takes his hand.)*
13   I had a dream about you.
14
15
16
17
18
19
20
21
22
23
24
25
26
27
28
29
30
31
32
33
34
35

Ain't I a Woman?
by Sojourner Truth
edited by Lydia Cosentino

1   Sojourner Truth   Adult

2

3   *Sojourner Truth, the legendary African-American freedom fighter*
4   *who was active in the abolition of slavery and the women's*
5   *rights movements, provides this electrifying and inspiring speech*
6   *of a mature, self-confident golden age woman. In this historically*
7   *authentic character portrait, Sojourner Truth's courage and*
8   *indomitable spirit reveal her to be a flesh-and-blood woman with*
9   *a warm but subtle sense of humor.*

10

11   Well, children, where there is so much racket, there
12 must be something out of kilter. I think that 'twixt the
13 Negroes of the South and the women at the North, all
14 talking about rights, the white men will be in a fix pretty
15 soon. But what's all this here talking about?

16   That man over there says that women need to be helped
17 into carriages, and lifted over ditches, and to have the best
18 place everywhere. Nobody ever helps me into carriages, or
19 over mud-puddles, or gives me any best place! And ain't I a
20 woman? Look at me! Look at my arm. I have ploughed and
21 planted, and gathered into barns, and no man could head
22 me! And ain't I a woman? I could work as much and eat as
23 much as a man — when I could get it — and bear the lash
24 as well! And ain't I a woman? I have borne thirteen children,
25 and seen them most all sold off to slavery, and when I cried
26 out with my mother's grief, none but Jesus heard me! And
27 ain't I a woman?

28

1   If the first woman God ever made was strong enough to
2   turn the world upside down all alone, these women together
3   ought to be able to turn it back, and get it right-side up again!
4   And now they is asking to do it, the men better let them.
5   Obliged to you for hearing me, and now old Sojourner ain't
6   got nothing more to say.
7
8
9
10
11
12
13
14
15
16
17
18
19
20
21
22
23
24
25
26
27
28
29
30
31
32
33
34
35

Looking for Love
by Jimmy Keary

1 Vivienne   Adult

2

3 *Vivienne Maxwell, a mature single woman, sits quietly at a small*

4 *table in a dimly-lit cafe and glances at her watch. Although she*

5 *has a successful professional career and exhibits all the social*

6 *graces of a sophisticated middle-age woman, Vivienne is lonely.*

7 *Having recently answered a lonely hearts personal ad, she is now*

8 *nervously waiting to meet the man in question in a late-night*

9 *Dublin, Ireland rendezvous.*

10

11 'Task, it's twenty five past and there's still no sign of

12 him! I wonder if he is coming at all. Maybe he got cold feet

13 at the last minute. I know I nearly did. God, maybe I gave

14 him the wrong directions! At this very moment he could be

15 in another Bewley's cafe, accosting some bewildered

16 female, who'll probably hit him with her handbag and call

17 the guards. No, I'm sure I told him this was the place — and

18 I gave him a detailed description of what I'd be wearing.

19 *(Takes a drink of coffee, savoring every drop.)*

20 By the way, my name is Vivienne — Vivienne Maxwell.

21 I'm forty years of age or thereabouts, and I work for the

22 Eastern Health Board. I'm one of those women you often

23 see walking earnestly down official corridors, wearing plain

24 suits and sensible shoes, and clutching batches of files to

25 their chests. It's a nice job and the salary is good. You

26 could say I'm comfortably well-off. *(Takes another drink of*

27 *coffee.)* Life couldn't be better really, except for one thing —

28 I don't have anyone to share it with. By 'anyone,' I mean a

29 man. I do get very lonely sometimes, especially since

1   Mother died last year. It'd be nice to have someone to come
2   home to in the evenings — someone with whom to share the
3   little trials and tribulations of the day. And then there's my
4   biological clock to consider — it's running very fast. And I do
5   so want to have children! I know they can be noisy and
6   troublesome — and smelly, but if they were mine, I'd love
7   them to bits! But will I ever see the day? I've been on the shelf
8   so long that I'm beginning to look distinctly dusty. Which
9   reminds me ... *(VIVIENNE picks up her handbag, opens it, and*
10   *takes out a mirror. She checks her appearance and puts the mirror*
11   *back in the bag. She puts down the bag and looks at her watch*
12   *again.)*
13   He's over fifteen minutes late! I'm beginning to think he's
14   not coming at all. I'll give him another five minutes — just in
15   case. Denis is his name, by the way. He's a Meath man and
16   has his own business. He likes good conversation, current
17   affairs, sport, and music. I'll admit I'm not mad about current
18   affairs, but as long as he wouldn't expect me to watch those
19   political programs on television with him, I could learn to live
20   with it. I answered his ad a few weeks ago — after giving the
21   matter a lot of thought. He phoned me last Monday evening. I
22   was stunned! We talked for a while and arranged this meeting.
23   *(Checks her watch again.)* You know, I'm all askew. One part of
24   me desperately wants him to turn up, while another part of me
25   is terrified of meeting him. I know he sounded nice on the
26   phone — and I didn't find it hard to talk to him. But what's
27   going to happen when I meet him face to face? All I'm afraid
28   of is that I'll be too tongue-tied to say a word to him. Come
29   on, Vivienne, calm down. Pull yourself together. *(Takes a deep*
30   *breath.)* That's better.
31   You see, I haven't had much experience of dealing with
32   men — well, not on a personal level. Mother saw to that!
33   Whenever I brought a young man home, he nearly had to
34   produce a certificate of road-worthiness before she'd let him
35   through the front door. Then she used to sit with us the whole

1 time — for fear our hormones would get the better of us.
2 Needless to say, none of them ever asked me out a second
3 time. I could have cheerfully strangled her sometimes. Don't
4 get me wrong — I'm not bitter. In fact, I loved her dearly,
5 despite all her little foibles. I never realized just how much
6 until she'd gone. *(Looks at her watch again and takes a deep*
7 *breath.)* Time's up, Denis! I'm not waiting any longer! *(Starts to*
8 *get up, but stops.)* But what if he turns up in a few minutes and
9 I'm not here? *(Gets up.)* If he was serious about meeting
10 someone, he'd have been here on time!
11
12
13
14
15
16
17
18
19
20
21
22
23
24
25
26
27
28
29
30
31
32
33
34
35

Picasso's Women
by Brian McAvera

1 Gaby Lespinasse   Adult
2
3 *Unlike the many other women in Pablo Picasso's life, the youthful*
4 *Gaby Lespinasse seems to have decided quite early in the*
5 *relationship that life with the flamboyant artist would not be a good*
6 *match. The attractive and intelligent Gaby weighed all her options*
7 *and opted for safety — with another man. We find her now at the end*
8 *of her life, looking back over time and recalling their relationship.*
9
10   As I lay dying, Herbert, my husband Herbert, read me
11 the pages of a William Faulkner novel. What novel? Use your
12 intelligence!
13   Herbert was an American, affluent, cultured, of course,
14 surprisingly so for an American, who fell in love with Paris,
15 knew everyone, and enjoyed both the traditional and the
16 new. He read all the latest writers, had a subscription to
17 *Transition*, and there wasn't a decent painter or printmaker
18 in Montparnasse whom he didn't know.
19   So he read me *As I Lay Dying*.
20   He knew I wouldn't concentrate, just as he knew that I
21 loved the sound of his voice. If he was speaking English you
22 could hear his Stamford accent. When he spoke French, it
23 was the French of Montparnasse, elegantly phrased,
24 precise, grammatically exact.
25   Pablo's was somewhat different.
26   Pablo thought in Spanish, translated into peculiar
27 French like a boy construing a difficult passage, and spoke
28 the elegant rhythms of my language with all the finesse of
29 a butcher hacking at a cadaver.

1
2   So you are thinking, who am I, and who is Herbert? Not —
3 who is Pablo ... Some bookends to the footnotes of the Picasso
4 story? Nonentities? Hangers-on to the Picasso legend?
5   Well ... maybe footnotes ... but we had sense.
6   Herbert was right.
7   He played the game, trusted me to make the right
8 decision. And I did.
9
10   What decision you ask?
11   Simple: Pablo asked me to marry him.
12   Well ... that is not quite correct. He asked me, then he
13 begged me. Again and again.
14   And I refused.
15   But more of that later.
16   I was the first person he asked to marry him ... but not the
17 last!
18
19   You see, I wasn't quite like Pablo's other women.
20   Oh, I don't mean to acquire airs and graces but my family,
21 while not being enormously rich, were more than comfortable.
22 I had an allowance for those early years, my own flat in the
23 Boulevard Raspail, top flat — fifth floor but my own flat — and
24 when I first met Pablo I already knew Herbert; had even taken
25 his name. So I had no absolute need to get a husband, no
26 panicky thoughts as to where the next baguette was coming
27 from, no need to bait a trap for lifelong security.
28
29   I was just being me.
30
31   Oh I know: you are asking yourselves, was she mad?
32   Why did she refuse the great God Pablo Picasso? Why
33 marry a nonentity like Herbert Lespinasse, an artist whom
34 most of the world has never heard of! Think of the money, the
35 fame ...

1   Well, think of it indeed. You only need so much money to
2   stay alive. What use is the rest? Look at me. Do I look as if
3   you can take it with you?
4   And fame? Well, what use is fame if it imprisons you?
5
6
7
8
9
10
11
12
13
14
15
16
17
18
19
20
21
22
23
24
25
26
27
28
29
30
31
32
33
34
35

Mothers Mary
by Paul Hancock

1   Mary   Young Adult/Adult
2
3   *In this contemporary version of the biblical Mary and Joseph*
4   *story, an angel attempts to cajole Mary into bearing a son ... but*
5   *to no avail. When the choice is taken away from her, Mary lapses*
6   *into an ecstasy of divine conception — or, was it just a dream?*
7   *Here, Mary sits and talks to the audience about her recent dream,*
8   *while she tries to change her appearance by applying makeup to*
9   *look older.*
10
11 Everyone says 'the world is a funny place,' 'people are
12 funny sometimes,' 'funny things can happen,' 'funny ... isn't
13 it?' But it's not really. The world is tragic — not all lives
14 are — but the world ... I don't understand why it is. We have
15 land, and food, and water. There is a lot of money about.
16 Many people know a lot of things. Still, it is. *(Beat.)*
17 And all our humor — it rises out of that. Ask yourself:
18 If I were so happy with my life, with the way things are
19 around me, the way events shape the world and its lives. If
20 I were happy with all of that, in that ideal moment, would I
21 need humor? We could laugh the pure laugh of a joyous
22 existence. But I guess we'll never see that. So, I can't prove
23 my theory. But then, well, if it did turn out that way, if it
24 could be like that, all the comedians would be put out of a
25 job. And they wouldn't be happy, would they? Already the
26 perfection is lost and we are back to where we started. *(A*
27 *beat.)* Irony is funny, isn't it?
28 *(A short pause.)* My brother died when I was very young.
29 I sometimes think about him ... and wonder what he

173

1 would've been like. My father died when I was 23. And Joe,
2 Joseph, my husband, he died too. I do miss him. A few years
3 ago my mother died. Perhaps that's just as well. Still, I keep
4 trying ... trying to figure out where everyone is going. *(A beat.)*
5 But — there is my son ... *my* son. *(Pause. Hesitates. Leans*
6 *toward the audience.)*
7 I had a dream last night. I almost always forget my
8 dreams. I've had many, I know that, but then I forget them.
9 Well ... except one. But, last night, I had a dream. There was
10 a baby, smiling at me. He was in my arms — his face close to
11 mine, the new breath warm against my skin. One hand held
12 gently to my neck while the other rested against my face. Can
13 you dream smells? I remember a sweet smell. Anyway, he
14 laughed once. Then he looked at me and spoke, in a soft
15 voice, words that were not of a child. 'Mother,' he said, 'I don't
16 want to leave.' And then he paused, till finally pressing his
17 head against my chest, I heard, 'I want to love you — but I'm
18 not allowed.' *(A moment.)*
19 He was gone. I searched but didn't see him anywhere.
20 Then I looked down, where he had been, and I saw the dark
21 red of blood upon my blouse. *(A long beat.)* Suddenly, I woke
22 up. *(MARY rises. Just before turning away she looks at the*
23 *audience.)* Dreams are funny sometimes ... aren't they?
24
25
26
27
28
29
30
31
32
33
34
35

Men & Cars
by Diane Spodarek

1 Maggie   Adult

2

3 *Maggie, a musician and single mother, perches seductively on a*
4 *stool at The Last Exit Bar. There is an uncertain charm about her,*
5 *and it is apparent that she is a unique woman of self-confidence*
6 *and strength of character. Maggie delights in the barroom*
7 *intrigues and scandals that make the nightly rounds, and here*
8 *she spins her own tall tale for the amusement of the patrons.*

9

10   I like to drink a tall Bud when I'm walking around the
11 streets of Manhattan. I keep it in a brown paper bag and sip
12 it through a straw. Sometimes I like to stand on the corner
13 and wait. Wait for the men. You ever watch men and their
14 cars? Ever watch men look under their cars? I like the way
15 men look when they look under their cars.
16   I like to watch men sit in their cars, start them up, find
17 out they don't start, get out, look at the car, then go to the
18 hood. Open the hood, look in, go back to the inside of the
19 car, and try to start it up again. Get out again, look under
20 the car, look at the ground, look at the spill on the ground,
21 look all around, sometimes at their companion, if they're
22 with someone. If not, look for another man in the vicinity to
23 share this moment. Then there are two or three sometimes
24 four men looking under the hood or looking under the car,
25 or at the ground. Sometimes they stare at the spill on the
26 ground together, and then they look at each other and they
27 get that look. I like that look. It's somehow familiar. I can't
28 put my finger on it, I can't really say what it is, but it just
29 gives me a funny feeling watching them, the men and their

1   cars, although I don't really think it has anything to do with
2   the fact that I'm from Detroit.
3
4
5
6
7
8
9
10
11
12
13
14
15
16
17
18
19
20
21
22
23
24
25
26
27
28
29
30
31
32
33
34
35

The Woman Who Turned into a Bear
by Kathleen Marie Connor

1 Nadine   Adult

2

3 *Nadine, a native woman, tells the gripping story of a white*
4 *woman who turned into a bear to save a child from a vicious*
5 *attack by a real bear. Sitting around a campfire late at night,*
6 *Nadine's tale has supernatural undertones. There is an air of*
7 *mystery and initial unease as Nadine begins her storytelling, but*
8 *her recollection is more a hymn of awe and fascination than a*
9 *simple retelling of the events she has witnessed.*

10

11   **Christie settled her two kids down on a blanket she**
12 **brought for a nap. They fell asleep I guess, then she came**
13 **over with the rest of the women for a smoke and cup of**
14 **coffee while we sorted the berries and just talked.** *(NADINE*
15 *exhales smoke from the cigarette she is smoking.)* **Christie**
16 **mostly listened, and looked over at her kids to make sure**
17 **they were still sleeping. We didn't notice, but two of the little**
18 **girls had crept away to go back picking berries. It was Mary**
19 **Cunningham's two — Lisa, the older one, and her little**
20 **sister Theresa, who was only two and a half and still in**
21 **diapers. So, we were talking and didn't even notice those**
22 **two little girls creep away quietly, with a little battered**
23 **bucket that they brought.** *(Pause. NADINE now takes a deep*
24 *drag from her cigarette. Then she speaks tensely.)*
25   **All of a sudden, we heard screaming. We could tell it**
26 **was a little girl and she was screaming bloody murder. We**
27 **just froze there — couldn't figure it out, and then everyone**

1 scrambled up, berries flying all over the blankets, and ran for
2 that screaming. *(Voice shaking.)* The bear had her, the little
3 one, and was dragging her away toward the bushes. *(Pause.*
4 *She draws her hand across her forehead as though she is seeing it*
5 *happen again right in front of her.)* It had her by the diaper, and
6 she was hanging limp. We could see blood on her head and
7 back. The big sister, Lisa, was just screaming and crying —
8 standing there with her arm bleeding 'cause she had tried to
9 grab Theresa away from the bear, we found out after. *(Takes a*
10 *drag off cigarette, slowly exhales and shrugs.)*
11   What could we do? None of us had a gun or anything
12 besides a little axe to chop campfire wood. We all stood rooted
13 to the ground. Lisa had stopped screaming, and it got quiet
14 and still — except for the sound of the bear grunting. Theresa
15 was sort of moaning, so we knew she was still alive. *(Pause.*
16 *NADINE looks off into space and speaks in a wondering tone of*
17 *voice.)* Then, it was the strangest thing. I felt a force, or a
18 power behind me — like an electric current in the air. And I
19 could feel the presence of something growing — big, high up
20 in the air. *(Pause. NADINE speaks in a quiet tone of voice.)* When
21 I looked behind me, Lisa was already staring at something
22 behind me, and the expression on her face was really
23 something. Terrified, but with a strange light on her face —
24 like those pictures you see in the Catholic church of the saints
25 seeing a vision. *(Pause.)* I know that Christie was right there
26 with us, even though her two kids were still sleeping on the
27 ground. I could hear her breathing heavily behind me after we
28 ran. I turned around ... and she ... she was growing, soaring
29 way up into the air. Towering above us — all furry, brown fur,
30 like a huge grizzly, with snarling teeth and huge, clawed paws.
31 And her eyes, they were looking at the other bear, and they
32 were mad, glowing red.
33   She had the power, and we didn't even know it. One
34 minute she was Christie, and the next minute she was a huge
35 brown bear. She moved forward, on her hind paws, swaying

1 her head and growling at the other bear. The black bear
2 dropped Theresa, who just lay there. It reared up on its hind
3 legs and swayed back and forth, sniffing the new bear's scent.
4 Then it kind of grunted, turned around and loped away into
5 the bushes. For a minute we were all too stunned, you know,
6 not quite sure what to do. Christie started to shrink down, and
7 the fur disappeared. Then she was just there, her normal
8 white woman self, and running toward the little girl.
9   *(Pause. Thoughtfully.)* I can still see it ... Christie turning into
10 a bear. It's like when you look directly at the sun at high noon.
11 You know, like they all tell you not to do, and you get that after
12 image behind your eyes, bright and searing. When I think about
13 it now, that was a typical woman thing that Christie did with her
14 power. She saw something that had to be done, a child had to
15 be saved from a bear; and she changed herself to do it. What
16 she did was on a level with the bear, one bear to another, and
17 it worked. It was the right use of her power at the time. She
18 just felt it, like a medicine woman would.
19
20
21
22
23
24
25
26
27
28
29
30
31
32
33
34
35

Soot and Sunshine
by Rita Sizemore Riddle

1 Narrator   Young Adult/Adult
2
3 *In this short narrative poem titled "Healing," a non-native narrator*
4 *recalls the popular backwoods and mountain folk potions and*
5 *remedies used to treat illness in the Appalachian region of the*
6 *southern states. The narrator is on an adventurous journey back*
7 *home as she finds comfort in recalling her father as a*
8 *compassionate and warm caregiver during childhood illnesses.*
9
10   Mama had lots of home remedies
11   for all kinds of homemade calamities:
12   warm pee water for scratches or sties,
13   ear wax for fever blisters,
14   three kinds of weeds or a snuff-spit swipe
15   for bee stings. She bought O. C. B. powder
16   for extra-deep cuts or scrapes, soaked rock
17   candy in whisky for colds and coughs,
18   pasted baking soda on a burn. She didn't buy
19   laxatives, as long as she had soap-sticks
20   and we'd sit still. Mama thought castor oil,
21   chased by corn bread,
22   cured everything.
23
24   Daddy didn't touch or treat us much, except
25   when we had briars or splinters in our hands.
26   He'd hold the hand, burn a needle
27   with a match or Ronson lighter. First he'd find
28   the tiny spear, then pull it out
29   with vice-grip nails, smoky with nicotine.

1   Best of all was an ear ache. Then my daddy
2   lifted me on his lap, bent his head to mine
3   laid his lips against my ear, and blew
4   hot tobacco smoke to ease the pain.
5   Whatever happened to us
6   before or after those times,
7   his breath in my ear
8   told me then
9   all I needed to know.
10
11
12
13
14
15
16
17
18
19
20
21
22
23
24
25
26
27
28
29
30
31
32
33
34
35

Stepping Out
by Richard Harris

1   Mavis   Adult

2

3   *Mavis, a self-confident ex-professional dancer with a flair for the*
4   *dramatic, volunteers to give lessons in a local church north of*
5   *London, England. The weekly tap dancing class attracts a group*
6   *of middle-age women and shy, reclusive men. Mavis faces quite*
7   *a challenge rehearsing this motley crew of aspiring performers for*
8   *the grand charity show performance!* .

9

10   Okay, everyone, let's get on, shall we? It's our first
11 rehearsal, so lots of concentration, yes? *(Indicating.)* **Rose,**
12 **Sylvia and Andy** — we'll take you three at the back — no,
13 **Rose** in the middle please. Then we'll have **Maxine, Vera,**
14 **Lynne and Dorothy** — spread yourselves out so you can be
15 seen. But come forward a step, you're crowding — and
16 **Geoffrey,** let's have you at the front, directly in front of
17 **Rose.**
18   Okay. So you're standing with your backs to the
19 audience ... *(She will demonstrate, turning her back to them.)*
20 Feet apart, and absolutely still — nothing moving. The
21 curtains or the lights come up or whatever and you stay
22 there, not moving, absolutely static still. For four counts you
23 do absolutely nothing.
24   On given counts, back line, middle line and **Geoffrey**
25 turn around and face the front. No, you don't move your feet
26 and so your legs are crossed ... From there you bring the
27 right arm up, leaving the left arm down, you lift the hat and
28 you hold it high — yes? On counts three and four, line of
29 four does exactly the same thing but when you turn you

1 leave the right arm down, holding the hat low. Incidentally,
2 there's going to be some fast bouncing around and you might
3 have bust troubles, so wear something good and firm, yes?
4 *(Generally.)* **Right. We'll have the first four bars and make sure**
5 **the intro is spot on — it's got to be good, it's got to have**
6 **panache, it's got to have the three T's. What are the three**
7 **T's? Tits, teeth and tonsils.**
8 *(Demonstrates.)* **You smile, you stick your chest out, you**
9 **look like you're enjoying it. You've only got two T's, haven't**
10 **you, Geoffrey? Okay, let's have you in your opening positions**
11 **and we'll try it again. Quick as you can, please Rose, we've**
12 **got to get through! Dorothy — just a little smaller ... Sylvia,**
13 **can we get rid of the gum? I want to see your teeth, not hear**
14 **them! All right? And it's five six seven eight ... Da da da dada**
15 **da middle line ... Sway, sway Geoffrey! Okay. I think the**
16 **problem is that when you turn, some of you are a little off**
17 **balance. Right, back into position please and we'll do it**
18 **again — other way round please, Sylvia — and it's five six**
19 **seven eight.** *(Demonstrates.)* **Then ... shuffle ball change,**
20 **shuffle ball change shuffle ball change, six tap springs and**
21 **hold. Right. Now, let's try it to the music!**
22
23
24
25
26
27
28
29
30
31
32
33
34
35

Perfection
by Deanna Riley Cain

1 Roxy   Young Adult/Adult

2

3 *Roxy, an attractive and slightly large woman, is offended when*
4 *she observes someone staring at her for no apparent reason.*
5 *Pausing, abruptly, to consider the situation, Roxy responds in a*
6 *stream of colorful chatter about the role of "denial" in helping her*
7 *achieve a sense of perfection. The social commentary is piercing,*
8 *but her wit is sharp and the message is direct.*

9

10   I am perfect. I know what you're thinking ... But you're
11 wrong. I'm right. Don't worry. Happens all the time. Despite
12 what most people think, you're not born perfect. Born with
13 a silver spoon, born on third base, born again, but not born
14 perfect. I was making myself miserable. Everywhere I
15 looked, I was wrong. Wasn't thin enough, tan enough, sexy
16 enough, smart enough, dumb enough. Miserable. Miserable.
17 Miserable. Couldn't cook, clean, or macramé holiday
18 placemats. Couldn't balance a checkbook or do math home-
19 work. My doctors were out of network, my cell phone was
20 out of range, and my computer was out of disc space. My
21 grocery line was the longest, my ATM was jammed, and my
22 dog had fleas. Again. My Christmas cards were never
23 addressed, written, or mailed. But I did buy the cards. My
24 favorite ice cream is vanilla. Plain vanilla. Not even French
25 vanilla.
26   Sometimes I would get a 'C+.' Average with extra effort.
27 Not perfect. Not even a perfect failure. Average. And I
28 wanted a change. I wanted to be on the 'A-list.' No waiting
29 at crowded restaurants. Tellers open their windows just for

1 me. Always having exact change. But how to make me
2 change? Where to look? How to start?
3   Then it came to me. Denial. Denial was the perfect
4 strategy. Now I can't claim credit for it because I wasn't perfect
5 at the time. My mother gave me the insight. My mother has
6 always had a fabulous figure, not perfect mind you, but very
7 good. Much better than mine to tell you the truth. Quite
8 voluptuous. As she has gotten a little older, she has put on a
9 few pounds and is not the size she used to be. But does she
10 acknowledge that? Not for one second. My mother explained to
11 me that she is wearing larger sizes because sizes were
12 originally designed around 1906 and American women were
13 smaller then. As advances in medicine, diet, and exercise have
14 progressed, American women have grown in size. So the
15 fashion designers all over the world got together to make
16 adjustments in sizes. Although she 'wears' a fourteen or
17 sixteen, she is 'still a size six.' The sizes got smaller and it's
18 because of the fashion designers' international conspiracy. My
19 mother is a very happy woman. She believes she is the same
20 size she was when she was twenty-two. Ignorance is bliss.
21 Denial is the way to happiness.
22   At first, I had a little trouble working in the denial. At the
23 bank, I cut in front of a six-foot-two, 210 pound woman.
24 Lesson one: Pick your denials carefully. The next time, I
25 pictured myself in the front of the line and everyone in front of
26 me was performance art. Very entertaining. No stress. They
27 actually paid me to see the performance. What more could I
28 want? Then the perfection started rolling. My steaks were
29 actually cooked medium rare and not something in between.
30 The ATM gave me an extra twenty. Got the cheapest long
31 distance coverage. Bought placemats. Balanced my
32 checkbook. Got a raise. Got two. Had groceries delivered at
33 home. Won a new computer. Dumped my old cell phone. My
34 dog's fleas left him for another dog. Felt taller, thinner, sexier.
35 And I started wearing pre-fashion conspiracy sizes. Vanilla

1   was the flavor of the week — for a month! Finally, I had
2   achieved perfection. Bliss.
3   There's only one impediment to total worldwide perfection.
4   I need you to help acknowledge that I'm perfect. 'Duchess of
5   Perfection. Queen of Denial.' *(Raises voice.)* While I reign
6   supreme, everyone will be happy. Perfection in every pot.
7   Denial at every door. 'Queen for a Day every day.' What a
8   success story. A 'C' is an 'A' in every way. Help me show
9   others how to use this gift. Ignorance is bliss. And everyone
10 wants to be happy. How can you deny me? I'm perfect.
11
12
13
14
15
16
17
18
19
20
21
22
23
24
25
26
27
28
29
30
31
32
33
34
35

One Hundred Women
by Kristina Halvorson

1   Nina   Young Adult/Adult
2
3   *Nina, a young adult of grace and charm, celebrates her emerging*
4   *womanhood with a sense of anticipation and quiet dignity. Her*
5   *courageous spirit reflects the emotional turmoil and mental anguish*
6   *of the "one hundred women" that live and breathe inside her. The*
7   *inner strength of these women is almost spiritual in its capacity to*
8   *help Nina define herself and to discover her own truthfulness.*
9
10   There is a place, inside me, where one hundred women
11 live. It is full of light and anything but lonely. I keep Kelly
12 there, and my mother, and my third-grade teacher, Mrs.
13 Rhodes, and my best friend, Christine, from eighth grade,
14 and all the other women who have touched me somehow.
15 There are so many. I close my eyes and I imagine them
16 sitting close together in interlocked circles, talking, holding
17 each other, laughing. Inside me, they know one another.
18 Perhaps some of them are the same. When I am alone I
19 laugh along with them, wrap my arms tight around my
20 breasts, hugging myself, drawing them closer to me.
21   It's only when the men invite themselves in — into the
22 room, into the laughter, even into me — that the links of this,
23 this woman chain are weakened. The men call, and the
24 women come. The circles break apart. I begin to feel like I am
25 coming apart, that my parts are loose and dangling. I hug
26 myself even tighter and rename, re-imagine my women. There
27 is at least one hundred of me, without them, I think — Nina
28 the scholar, Nina the poet, the student, the counselor, the
29 lover. I wait for the strongest one of me to step forward so

1   that I can find the right words, summon up the elusive courage
2   to bring back the women I've somehow lost.
3   And yet, despite my frantic attempts to call forth the
4   philosopher, the diplomat, the encouraging friend, somehow it
5   is always Nina the lover who wins out. She gives into the
6   romance, releases the women to their princes and saviors. Her
7   mother remarries, her schoolteacher moves away with her
8   husband, her best friend falls head over heels for a ninth grader.
9   And Nina the lover nods; Nina the lover knows. She lowers her
10   head and waits for her turn to come, and in the meantime the
11   women fall away from her one by one by one ...
12   What can I do but embrace her, this lover who lives inside
13   my chest; and bid farewell to the other ninety-nine of me, who
14   always retreat in silence. How difficult can it be to call out the
15   name of a friend you're terrified of losing?
16
17
18
19
20
21
22
23
24
25
26
27
28
29
30
31
32
33
34
35

They Say I'm Obsessive
by Nancy Gall-Clayton

1 Vivian   Young Adult/Adult
2
3 *A number-loving young woman exhibits all the comic traits of*
4 *obsessive behavior while dining out at a local restaurant. The*
5 *character sketch has an amusing point of view and offers an*
6 *ingenious response when the diner realizes she has no money to*
7 *pay for her meal. Although the diner is good-humored and warm-*
8 *spirited, there may be more here than mere surface appearances.*
9
10   I have a question about my bill if you have just a
11 minute. Some people say I'm obsessive, but actually, I just
12 happen to love numbers. I love the way they line up from the
13 beginning of time to the end of time. I love my telephone
14 number and my address and my nine-digit zip code. I love
15 my social security number and the numbers on tax forms.
16   When it is permitted, and unfortunately it isn't always, I
17 use numbers and numbers alone for passwords. I love
18 counting things, like my socks which I count by two's, and
19 my dogs of which I have one, and my books, which currently
20 number 315. I also love to count money, and that relates to
21 the problem I want to mention to you.
22   I counted my money quite recently, and it seems I have
23 only 87 cents. I already ate the burger and fries and I drank
24 down the big tall glass of iced tea. I've been to the ladies'
25 room and looked in my socks (both of them), my pockets
26 (all three), my bra (both sides) and all the other places
27 where I occasionally leave large bills in case someone steals
28 my purse. I was going to offer to wash dishes, thinking how
29 much fun it would be to count them, but then I remembered

1 that I don't have a copy of my latest chest x-ray, and besides,
2 I might do it wrong and ruin a valuable knife or spatula.
3   So what to do? One possibility is stand on the corner and
4 tout the food at this eating establishment to each and every
5 passerby. At minimum wage, I could work an hour and twenty-
6 three minutes, and we'd be even except for the tip. And, don't
7 worry, I could not sleep if I did not leave a tip. I usually leave
8 18%, trying to do my fair share to end the stereotype of the
9 solo female diner stiffing the wait staff. Eighteen is a lucky
10 number if you're Jewish, which I'm not, but still. And I tip on
11 the whole amount after taxes have been added in, so I prefer
12 the adjective generous over the adjective obsessive, but alas,
13 at this moment, neither adjective can be applied to me. So,
14 with your permission and that of the other seven servers if you
15 need their agreement, I will leave. If you need me, you'll find
16 me on the corner of 4th and Chestnut. Here's your 87 cents
17 and thank you very much.
18
19
20
21
22
23
24
25
26
27
28
29
30
31
32
33
34
35

After the Garden
by Robert J. Lee

1 Eve and Adam   Young Adults/Adults

2

3   *Duolog*

4   *Here is a partner duolog that offers a fresh interpretation of*

5   *the familiar biblical characters Adam and Eve. Although*

6   *this adaptation focuses on the despair and isolation*

7   *following expulsion from the Garden of Eden, there are witty*

8   *exchanges of dialog that suggest each character's emerging*

9   *sense of humor. These characters are more human than their*

10   *historical role models, especially when they are saying*

11   *outrageous things or gently teasing each other. In playing*

12   *the scene, carefully blend your own distinctive personality*

13   *traits with those of the characters to give added meaning to*

14   *the surface details described. Remember that what is said or*

15   *done is not nearly as potentially comic as how it is said or*

16   *done. So explore the comic subtext in each character's vocal*

17   *or physical responses through an imaginative use of facial*

18   *expressions, pauses, mannerisms, and gestures.*

19

20   *Adam and Eve stumble forward from behind some bushes*

21   *and face each other Center Stage. Eve wears a look of*

22   *agitated displeasure and Adam masks a frown of despair.*

23   *The downcast appearances mirror the depth of each*

24   *character's isolation following their recent expulsion from*

25   *the Garden of Eden. Against this bittersweet backdrop,*

26   *Adam and Eve fall victim to the first recorded "family spat."*

27

28 ADAM: Well, this will be a good excuse to do some

29   traveling. Don't get me wrong the garden was nice and

1   all but it's good for us to get away together. Which way
2   should we go first? How about west? *(Points toward*
3   *audience. EVE keeps walking.)* Okay, north is good. Eve,
4   you haven't said two words in the past four hours. Is
5   there something wrong? *(Silence.)* Are you mad? *(EVE*
6   *stops. Turns and glares at him.)* What's wrong? Did I do
7   something? *(Tries to take her hand but she jerks it away.)*
8   What did I do? *(EVE turns and heads Stage Left.)* Come on
9   you've got to at least let me know what I did wrong. Did
10   I say something wrong? *(Stops and stares.)* What?
11 EVE: You know what you said.
12 ADAM: How should I know what I said if you won't tell me?
13 EVE: I might just never speak to you again.
14 ADAM: What did I say?
15 EVE: *(Mockingly.)* That woman You gave me, she gave me of
16   the tree, and I ate.
17 ADAM: I didn't say that.
18 EVE: You most certainly did!
19 ADAM: I did not.
20 EVE: Look it up.
21 ADAM: Huh?
22 EVE: Genesis 3:12.
23 ADAM: Okay, but I didn't really mean it like it sounded. I only
24   meant that ...
25 EVE: Don't try to weasel your way out of it. You never want
26   to give me credit for helping, but just let one little thing
27   go wrong and ...
28 ADAM: One little thing huh? You call breaking the only rule
29   we had one little thing?
30 EVE: Not so fast there buster. Who told you, you had to listen
31   to me in the first place? Did I hold you down and shove
32   that fruit down your throat?
33 ADAM: So I thought I told you not to hang around with the
34   serpent.
35 EVE: Well, he tricked me.

1 ADAM: Well there you go then. I wonder why he didn't come
2   around trying to tempt me?
3 EVE: Probably because he figured you couldn't reach the fruit.
4 ADAM: Hey wait a minute!
5 EVE: But besides, who said this was about me? Don't you try
6   to change the subject.
7 ADAM: Uh not so loud Eve. We really shouldn't be fighting
8   like this in front of the kids.
9 EVE: We don't have any kids.
10 ADAM: Oh. That's right. Well ...
11 EVE: So if you think you can humiliate me in front of God like
12   that and get away with it you've got another thing coming
13   Mister. Not even a thought to my feelings.
14 ADAM: But Honey ...
15 EVE: Don't you 'But Honey' me, you ...
16 ADAM: But Sugar if you'll just ... *(Tries to take her hand.)*
17 EVE: I wouldn't let you touch me if you were the only man
18   on ... Oh. Well never mind, just keep your hands off me.
19 ADAM: Come on Eve, how long are you going to stay mad like
20   this? *(EVE is silent.)* Look, I'll make it up to you.
21 EVE: Hmmph!
22 ADAM: Well ... I'll toil the ground for you. You won't have to
23   do any of the dirty stuff.
24 EVE: Sure like that's your idea. We both know that God's
25   making you do that. Tell you what ... How about if we
26   change assignments. I'll toil the earth and you give birth
27   in pain.
28 ADAM: *(Thinks.)* I don't know, don't you think He's mad at us
29   enough as it is?
30 EVE: *(Grudgingly.)* Yeah you're right.
31 ADAM: O.K., look I won't leave clothes lying around and I'll
32   sweep the dirt. I won't make any mother-in-law jokes.
33   Just please give me a hug.
34 EVE: Can I name the kids?
35 ADAM: Well, I don't know ...

1 EVE: Hey, you got to name all the animals!
2 ADAM: You weren't even here yet! I was handling everything all
3   my myself y'know. *(Under his breath.)* **Sure was peaceful.**
4 EVE: What was that?
5 ADAM: Oh uh, I was just reminding myself how lonely it was.
6   Okay Honey, how 'bout if we name the kids together.
7 EVE: Well, okay. But I get to name the first one.
8 ADAM: How about we flip for it. C'mon let's go talk about
9   baby names. Hey, what's for dinner? *(Heads Stage Left.)*
10 EVE: *(Watches him leave, shakes her head.)* **That woman You**
11   **gave me!**
12 ADAM: Why is this itching so much? Aaughh! Eve, where did
13   you get these leaves?
14 EVE: *(Faces audience with mischievous grin and then heads Off-*
15   *stage.)* **Adam? What's a mother-in-law?**
16
17
18
19
20
21
22
23
24
25
26
27
28
29
30
31
32
33
34
35

New Age Voices

That is happiness: to be dissolved into
something complete and great.

— *Willa Cather,* Reflections

The monolog characters in this chapter were written especially for classroom performances or auditions and are not excerpts from longer scripts. One of the challenges for you is to discover inventive approaches to characterization, interpretation, and staging without a complete script to provide additional character clues. With the practical experience and knowledge already gained through script analysis, you should now be able to identify performance strategies for these independent stage figures as well.

New age character voices share many of the life experiences, personal opinions, and points of view expressed by other monolog characters in this collection. They are incisive and vivid characters that have distinct lifestyles, idiosyncrasies, and personalities. Some of the characters may have emerged as an adaptation from a novel, diary, short story, screenplay, or one-person narrative sketch by the author. Although these monologs are not from specific acts or scenes of complete scripts, they are still inspired and insightful character sketches that will leave a memorable impression in classroom performances or auditions. Each monolog isolates a central performance moment and indicates character conflict. Each monolog also stimulates vocal and physical interaction with other imaginary characters, generates active stage business, and offers a variety of character ages, vocal ranges, and physical types.

In playing these excerpts, it may be a good idea to keep in mind a brief outline of character actions or reactions suggested in the monolog. Then improvise individual character moments of stage business to better understand the desire or motivation of these abbreviated stage figures. You should pay some attention to the opportunities presented for movement, bodily action, or gestures that help complete the monolog character portrait. You should also indicate in your introduction that the excerpt is an independent monolog, and not part of a longer script. Once you have explored the creative character-building possibilities of these new age voices, your theatrical mind should be attuned to any audition or performance challenge!

The Baptist Gourmet
by Jill Morley

1 Tulula   Young Adult/Adult
2
3 *Tulula, a fun-loving Southern belle and galloping gourmet, hosts*
4 *a cooking show on cable television. She dispenses culinary*
5 *secrets and juicy tidbits of gossip like salt and pepper to whet the*
6 *tastebuds of the small town wives who watch her show.*
7
8 G'Morin'! Welcome to Channel 64's *Cooking with Tulula.*
9 I'm Tulula Lee May, your Baptist Gourmet and before I lead
10 you in a recipe, I'm gonna lead you in a prayer.
11   Lordy, Lordy, let me learn. Not to let my souffle burn.
12 And if it does, ohhh promise me this. Someone in my
13 kitchen will like it crisp! Amen.
14   Last night, I was divinely inspired when the Lord came
15 to me in a dream and He said, 'Tulula, you are my culinary
16 link to humanity. I bestow upon you the celestial
17 preparation for fried grits.'
18   Ingredients are hominy, cheese, and the life-giving
19 energy to all the Lord's creatures ... fat.
20   First you must baptize your ingredients. *(Throws water*
21 *on the ingredients with fervor.)* You're baptized! You're
22 baptized! You're baptized!
23   Next, we finely chop the hominy and the cheese, which
24 I already have done because they won't let me have the air
25 time I need. *(Smiles and winks at a producer Off-stage.)* Isn't
26 that right, Jimmy? *(Under her breath.)* Producer Shmoducer.
27   Then, we take the hominy, the cheese, we put it in a
28 skillet and FRY IT UP! JUST FRY IT UP! IN THE NAME OF
29 THE LORD, JUST FRY IT UP! *(Lightheaded, she sits down*

1   *and fans herself.)* **Oh, this is gonna be a good one.**
2   **Now, while we're waitin' for the culinary miracle, like**
3   **waitin' for the second coming, I'd like to read some of my**
4   **viewer mail. Preacher Mapplethorpe writes, 'Dear Tulula,**
5   **thank you for bringing that fried Caesar's salad to the church**
6   **bazaar last week. Everyone raved over those cute little baby**
7   **Jesus croutons. And that parmesan cheese looked like snow**
8   **in the manger!' Amen.**
9   **Tessie Jo Miller from Duncan Road asks, 'Dear Tulula,**
10   **what is the rule of thumb in Southern Baptist food**
11   **preparation?' Tessie, has your cheese dun slid off your**
12   **cracker? Just slap on some cheese and FRY IT UP! FRY IT**
13   **UP! IN THE NAME OF THE LORD, JUST FRY IT UP!**
14   *(Collapses and fans herself again.)* **Lord save us all.**
15   **Letter from Madge Peeker on Winston Lane, 'How do I**
16   **make my home fried taters taste like yours?' Madge, I seen**
17   **the way you fry those taters at the church socials. You just**
18   **chop 'em all up like they was the devil's spawn! With each**
19   **slice, you must instill goodness and ethics and morality.**
20   **Handle your taters the way God handles His children and your**
21   **creation will be as perfect as His. On that note, let's resurrect**
22   **those grits ...** *(She tastes them.)* **Mmmmmmm, mmmmmmm,**
23   **just like the Lord woulda made them.**
24   **Now, tell your Catholic friends to tune in next week**
25   **because I'm making fried St. Joan Kabobs! Bye, y'all!**
26
27
28
29
30
31
32
33
34
35

Bell Bottoms
by Colleen Anderson

1 Woman   Adult
2
3 *A former "flower child" of the '70s, now a conservative middle-*
4 *aged woman, recalls her favorite pair of blue jeans and some*
5 *of the places she wore them in the search for personal freedom*
6 *and liberty.*
7
8   Everything goes in cycles. I saw some college kids
9 wearing bell-bottom jeans the other day, and it brought
10 back a rush of memory: my raggle-taggle, threadbare,
11 bleached-out bell-bottom blue jeans from 1970. I wore them
12 skin-tight and patched them wherever they gave out — and
13 whenever I got around to it — with calico scraps from Cabin
14 Creek Quilts, where I was working at the time.
15   I knew them from the inseam out. That was my hippie
16 year, the year I escaped from my Midwestern hometown and
17 landed in the West Virginia coal fields, the year I refused to
18 wear underwear. I washed them in Cabin Creek water that
19 ran red from acid mine waste and dried them outdoors on a
20 clothesline.
21   In the summer I hitchhiked all the way to Princeton, New
22 Jersey, alone, wearing those blue jeans, to visit my friend
23 Patty.
24   I remember digging in the tight pockets for cigarette
25 money, and dragging the hems through mud on the dirt
26 lanes of dying coal towns. As if in an old movie, I can watch
27 my younger self walk across Lena Hawkins' rope bridge,
28 wearing those jeans and a strange, peasant-y tunic I made
29 from a pattern of my own devising, and a pair of black, high-

1 topped sneakers I'd left sitting too long on the space heater
2 in the co-op, so that when I lifted them off, the rubber pulled
3 away and formed winged feet like Mercury's.
4   I can remember sitting on my knees, for hours, tapping the
5 rhythms of banjos and fiddles into the threadbare thighs of
6 those faded pants. I remember getting up and dancing in
7 them.
8   But I don't remember buying those blue jeans. I can't
9 believe I did buy them. They were mythical, magical, and they
10 must have come from some giveaway bin, with someone else's
11 wild history already in their legs.
12   For years and years, long past the days of bell-bottoms,
13 long after Lena was dead and I'd moved out of Cabin Creek, I
14 couldn't bear to throw them out. Even now, I don't know
15 where they are. They left me as mysteriously as they came,
16 and they're just gone, like being young is gone.
17
18
19
20
21
22
23
24
25
26
27
28
29
30
31
32
33
34
35

The Cost of Independence
by Robin Williams

1 Woman   Young Adult/Adult
2
3 *An African-American woman in her mid-thirties quietly reflects on*
4 *the cost of her independence. She offers a sensitive look at what it*
5 *means for a self-sufficient woman to sacrifice companionship,*
6 *friendship, and family ties to maintain her sense of pride.*
7
8   As a woman in my mid-thirties, I find myself thinking
9 about my independence. Growing up my mother taught me
10 the key to independence. She would say, 'You have to
11 provide for yourself out here, no man is going to do it for
12 you.' In learning that, I have been on my own and
13 independent for the last twenty years. Yes ... it has been
14 good at times ... but more than that, it has cost me some
15 valuable relationships. Men don't want an independent
16 woman, rather ... a dependent. To get involved with a
17 woman like me is to take on a challenge, one that men are
18 not ready or even willing to do. The cost of my
19 independence has been good relationships. I attract bad
20 men ... men who want nothing more out of life than to get
21 involved with a woman who has her head on straight, knows
22 where she is headed in life, and has the means to get there.
23 They want a mother figure ... someone who can take care of
24 them. In my mother's day, an independent woman was a
25 curse. I believe that same curse stands true today. Men
26 look at me and decide in their minds what measures to take
27 to break me down ... they want me to surrender all I am and
28 all that I have become ... to them. They want to take credit
29 for my success ... they want to be responsible for my

1   demise. Independence has given me some lonely days ... and
2   nights ... No one wants to associate themselves with a ready
3   made woman ... a woman who is not afraid to live below her
4   means ... a woman who can take on the role of husband and
5   wife ... father and mother ... a woman who can call her own
6   shots ... make her own dreams come true ... fight her own
7   battles without the help of a man. A woman who is
8   independent ... and is costly most ... to a man's life.
9
10
11
12
13
14
15
16
17
18
19
20
21
22
23
24
25
26
27
28
29
30
31
32
33
34
35

Sister Santa
by Jim Chevallier

1 Sister Santa   Teen/Young Adult
2
3 *In this dark parody of the Yuletide hero Santa Claus, Sister Santa*
4 *is a feisty and sour holiday elf. There is no merry Christmas spirit*
5 *or holiday cheer in Sister Santa's mocking tone as she taunts the*
6 *startled children standing in line to visit.*
7
8   Ho, ho, ho!
9   I am too Santa Claus, kid. Yeah, I'm a girl. Like duh — uh.
10 Because I need the money, O.K.? It's either you little germ-
11 donors or cooking Christmas burgers at the local take-out.
12   Hey, but enough about me. What greedy little totally
13 unreasonable demand do you want to make of the Great
14 White Beard? No, I didn't grow the beard. I'm a girl, O.K.?
15 We don't as a general thing grow beards. Hey, look, would
16 you rather have me or some red-eyed wino who's working
17 off his last bottle of Boone's Farm? Like liquor-breath, do
18 you? Well, then, work with me here, O.K.? I got midterms
19 next week plus a female problem you don't want to know
20 about, so trust me, I am not in the mood.
21   What'll it be then? A molded plastic semi-automatic so
22 you can imitate your favorite mad gunman? Some blood-
23 thirsty boy doll that crawls around on its belly, armed to the
24 teeth? A little remote control tank you can send shooting
25 through pedestrians' feet and scare the Pampers off frail old
26 ladies? Come on, sweetie, you just tell Sister Santa here
27 what violence and mayhem disguised as a toy will put your
28 little testosterone-tainted heart all a flutter. Rat-a-tat-tat!
29 Boom, boom, boom!

1   No, I do NOT have a problem with men! Where do you get
2 this stuff? What kind of shows do your parents let you watch,
3 anyway? And no there is nothing weird about a female Santa!
4 You better get used to it, kid, when you grow up, there's gonna
5 be girls EVERYWHERE! Yeah, that's right, we're even in the
6 Army!
7   Ah no, now I've gone and made you cry. Hey, can we get
8 a nurturer over here? Anyone into being maternal? Geez ...
9
10
11
12
13
14
15
16
17
18
19
20
21
22
23
24
25
26
27
28
29
30
31
32
33
34
35

Communications Management
by Jill Elaine Hughes

1 Louise   Adult
2
3 *Louise is a middle-age secretary to a busy executive, who*
4 *happens to be having an extramarital affair. Louise, who files her*
5 *nails and reads Martha Stewart's books while working at her*
6 *desk, must conceal the affair when the wife calls.*
7
8   Good afternoon, you have reached Stellar Electronics
9 Corporation, Philip Philipson's office. This is Louise
10 speaking. Oh, hello there Mrs. Philipson! How are you? How
11 are the kids? Oh. Oh I see. No ma'am, Mr. Philipson is out
12 of the office today on business. Well I assure you, ma'am he
13 is not here. Nope, not here right now. Well he's on a
14 business trip, don't you recall? Well I believe he is at his
15 hotel at the moment — er ahh, he is at the business ahhh,
16 yes, the hotel, umm-hmmm. No, I'm afraid I don't have the
17 number of his hotel just yet — he wasn't sure where he
18 would be staying — those conventions you know, the hotels
19 fill up so fast.
20   Well, yes it is usually my job to book his hotel, but you
21 do understand Mrs. Philipson that these are extraordinary
22 times we are living in today and — well — wait — but — oh
23 Mrs. Philipson! Now there's no reason to be taking that tone
24 with me, darling dear. Whatever I can do to help you, I will.
25 *(Pause.)* Well, as you surely know, Mr. Philipson is away on
26 a business trip until tomorrow afternoon, but he is calling in
27 for messages. Can I just take it down for you and have him
28 return the call? Well I am absolutely sure Mr. Philipson
29 would have told you all about the nature of his trip in great

1   detail. I don't mean to pry into your marriage or anything like
2   that but I am sure he would have told you everything, probably
3   just last evening before you went to bed. *(Pause.)*
4   He didn't? Well, then Mrs. Philipson I am sure you just
5   plumb forgot. What is the nature of his trip? Well, it is of a
6   business nature, I assure you. Very important, private
7   business. *(Pause.)* Well well well, I believe, it is to meet with the
8   ahhh, the ahhhh *(She flips through a thesaurus.)* General
9   Secretary for ... ahhhh, Social Events Management? Ahhhh,
10 which company? Oh at, ahhhh, Social Enterprises. Yes. Well,
11 they're ahhhh, they're a hospitality company. They give
12 hospitality to ... people. Well, their CEO is a very nice lady by
13 the name of, ahhhh *(She picks up her magazine.)* Martha
14 Stewart. Umm-hmm. Yes, he is in a business meeting with
15 Martha Stewart. Right now. In Hawaii. About? Ahhhh ...
16 Bedspreads. Her new line of bedspreads and sheets.
17   Well I realize that home fashions is a new line of business
18 for Stellar Electronics, Mrs. Philipson, but I'm sure you
19 already know that your husband is an extremely innovative
20 businessman. He has this idea for vibrating bed — sheets?
21 Oh, dear — well just forget I said that — what I really meant
22 was electric blankets. Yes, that's it, electric blankets. Oh now
23 Mrs. Philipson you really — oh darling dear, don't cry
24 sweetheart. It's just a business trip ma'am, you're husband
25 will be back home to you soon. *(Pause.)* Now ma'am, don't say
26 that. Oh, don't say that honey. I am sure that your husband
27 loves you very much. Oh he's always saying here in the office
28 about how much he loves his wife and kids. Now you just
29 hang up the phone and take yourself a nice hot bath Mrs.
30 Philipson and I'll tell your husband you called. Bye now.
31
32
33
34
35

Short and Sweet
by Willie Reale

1   Two Women   Youthful/Teens

2

3   *Here are two "short and sweet" monologs for young women that*

4   *have a genuine comic tone. The characters may be struggling to*

5   *realize their youthful dreams, but along the way they also*

6   *discover a very strong sense of self-identity.*

7

8   **The Problem Is Pickles**

9

10   I just broke up with my boyfriend. It's not like a big deal

11 or anything. I mean we didn't even go out on dates or to the

12 movies or something. It was just one of those, 'I like you,

13 you like me — let's be boyfriend and girlfriend.' He is

14 extremely cute, but the problem is pickles. He loves pickles.

15 He keeps a jar of half sour dills in his desk at school. You

16 can hear him crunching and slurping right there in math

17 class. You'll be doin' a problem and you hear: jar open,

18 crunch crunch slurp slurp jar close. Who can concentrate?

19 But the worst of it is the pickle smell. That was the deal

20 breaker. See before the end of the marking period, I'm

21 gonna kiss somebody. That's a little deal I made with

22 myself, the time has come, I'm the right age. It's gonna be

23 my first kiss and I'll always remember it and I tell you what,

24 it's not gonna be all about smelling like pickles. I'm not

25 having that. No sir.

26

27   **Holding Hand in a Hanky**

28

29   Stitches and a scar. All to open a can of tuna fish. I bet

1   the scar is ugly too. I mean here we are in this podunk hospital.
2   I'll get some twenty-one-year-old resident who's gonna be like,
3   'Oh goody I never done stitches before.' The scar will be ugly.
4   I will be permanently disfigured. Hand modeling, there's
5   another career out of my reach. I read somewhere that people
6   who have nice hands can make a fortune just to be
7   photographed holding up products. Here's ten thousand dollars
8   to hold up a frankfurter, here's another ten thousand to hold
9   up a box of Wheat Thins, here's twenty grand to wrap your
10 fingers around a canister of flea powder. Hand modeling. Just
11 add that to the list of careers I'll never have. Right up there
12 with professional athlete of any kind, all fields which require
13 math or science, anything to do with customer service or
14 people skills, anything requiring strength or coordination. I
15 think that leaves assembly line work or a career in the arts.
16 And the kicker is: I don't even like tuna fish.
17
18
19
20
21
22
23
24
25
26
27
28
29
30
31
32
33
34
35

Billie Sue's Statement
by T. W. McNemar

1   Billie Sue   Young Adult/Adult
2
3   *Billie Sue Diggs, an African-American woman in a small West*
4   *Virginia town, is taken into custody for assaulting her husband*
5   *and a police officer. In her recorded statement for the local*
6   *investigator, Billie Sue tries to explain her actions.*
7
8   Now, I jus' talk in this lil thing here? I can do that an', I
9   wanna thank ya'll fer being so nice to me an' my baby down
10 here. Now I guess you be wantin' me to say my piece 'bout
11 what happened out there this afternoon. Well, it's like this.
12   Pokey been with me longer than my baby's daddy was
13 around, oh I reckon 'bout nine ten month. Now he's a good
14 boy. He good to me an' real good to the baby, 'cept when
15 he drink. Now when the boy drink, he gets verbal, if you
16 know what I mean. Now he gets nasty. Well, he started on
17 me an' my butt this afternoon an' neither me nor my butt
18 was up to this. He said if Playboy was ta do a centerfold,
19 now they'd hafta do a aerial picture of me. Then he jus'
20 kept going till I got mad enough ta stomp him, an' well, you
21 know what happened. Then when ol' Junie Smith come in
22 that first police car an' pulled me offa him, he jump up with
23 his bloody nose an' swoll lips an' sayin' it a good thang ya'll
24 come when ya' did or she'da killed me? Why, Lord, that jus'
25 went through me, an' well … that's why I drop kick him …
26 an' I'm sorry 'bout knockin' Junie down an' all, so I am.
27   Now 'T' you know I'm a good God-fearin' woman an'
28 now, I'll jus' run Pokey off so he'll not be gettin' mouthy
29 with me no more, 'cause I can't do no more jail time on

1 'count o' the baby'd go to the county an' that'd break my
2 heart. Now you know I don't allow my lazy, crack-smokin'
3 brother 'round neither. I done whupped him there in March o'
4 this year an' he ain't been back neither ... you know ... on
5 account o' what you said last year. Now I don't think Pokey'll
6 be pressin', but you gotta let him sleep it off an' then, let me
7 talk to him ... you know what I'm saying, 'T?

8   My Mama was right 'bout men. She said they's like
9 grapes. You gotta stomp it out of 'em til they turn inta
10 somethin' acceptable ta have dinner with. You can turn the
11 thang off 'T,' I gonna stop talkin' now.
12
13
14
15
16
17
18
19
20
21
22
23
24
25
26
27
28
29
30
31
32
33
34
35

Hollywood 101
by Chambers Stevens

1 Brittany and Caroline   Teens
2
3 *There is a sense of reckless high spirits in these monologs that*
4 *offer a good-humored glimpse of the zany adventures of two*
5 *clever young teens. The style here is broad, but the savage*
6 *lampoon on "fashion police" and "open mike night" is hilarious!*
7
8   **Brittany**
9   **The Fashion Police**
10
11   *(BRITTANY comes running in, blowing her whistle.)*
12   Hold it! Yeah you with the orange jacket! Stop!
13 *(BRITTANY walks up to the fashion victim.)* I've already warned
14 you once this week, so I'm sorry, but I'm going to have to
15 give you a ticket. I mean, come on girl. An orange jacket
16 and a purple top? Where did you learn fashion? And those
17 socks. They don't even match ... each other. One is canary
18 yellow and the other one is more sunflower. Come on, this
19 is not the circus.
20   Speaking of clowns, you're wearing way, way too much
21 make-up. What do you put it on with, a paint brush? You
22 must have a whole tube of lipstick on those lips. Make-up
23 is supposed to enhance your beauty, not obliterate it. And
24 your mascara is way too heavy. You look like you were
25 running without a sports bra and you gave yourself two
26 black eyes.
27   Speaking of bras, not only is your strap showing but so
28 is the hair under your arms which you FORGOT TO SHAVE!
29 This is not the sixties! Buy yourself a razor. *(She writes out*

211

1   *the ticket.)* **You have so many infractions I can't fit them all on**
2   **one ticket. I'm going to have to take you in. Maybe this time**
3   **you'll learn what good taste is. Next time you decide to leave**
4   **the house, remember, the fashion police are watching you!**
5
6   Caroline
7   Sing Your Problems Away
8
9   *(CAROLINE walks on stage with her guitar. Even though her*
10 *songs are silly, she takes them very seriously.)*
11   **Hello. My name is Caroline Kryenski. And I guess you can**
12 **tell from my guitar that I'm a singer. Sorry if I'm a little**
13 **nervous, but this is my first open mike. My first song is about**
14 **my dog, Fluffy, who was recently run over by a car. It's called**
15 **'Fluffy Watch Out!'** *(She sits down, strums a few chords, and*
16 *starts to sing.)*
17   **Fluffy.**
18   **You're so cute running in the street.**
19   **Oh, no! A car!**
20   **Now Fluffy is flat!**
21   **Fluffy!**
22   **You're splattered on the street!**
23   **Looks like I'm going to have to get a cat.**
24   **Fluffy.**
25   **Watch out!**
26   *(Applause.)* **Thank you. Music has always been my dream.**
27 **Actually I had a great dream last night. My head was this**
28 **pumpkin and I kept spitting out the seeds. But that's another**
29 **story. My next song is dedicated to my ex-boyfriend, Zack,**
30 **otherwise known as the jerk who dumped me.**
31   *(Singing.)* **Zack.**
32   **You're a jerk.**
33   **A big jerk.**
34   **A huge jerk.**
35   **A massive jerk.**

1   **Zack. Zack. Zack.**

2   **Jerk. Jerk. Jerk.**

3   *(She plays a big chord and then stands to take a bow.)* **You are**

4 **too kind. Okay. My next song isn't really a song. It's more of**

5 **a dance. It's called: 'Fluffy comes back from the dead and**

6 **beats up Zack.'**

7   *(CAROLINE lies on the floor. She jumps up like a dog. Then she*

8 *runs to the other side of the stage and plays Zack lifting weights.*

9 *Then she turns into Fluffy again. Slowly Fluffy sneaks up on Zack.*

10 *CAROLINE runs back and forth on the stage doing a wild dance*

11 *playing both Fluffy and Zack. It ends with a wild fight scene.*

12 *CAROLINE is both victim and bully. When it is over she takes a*

13 *grand bow.)*

14   **Thank you, thank you. Well, my time is up. I'll be here next**

15 **week when I'm going to be performing my new song, 'Peanut**

16 **Butter is a great face cream.' Thank you.**

17

18

19

20

21

22

23

24

25

26

27

28

29

30

31

32

33

34

35

Angela
by Christine Emmert

1   Angela   Teen

2

3   *Angela, an angry teenager in serious need of psychological*
4   *counseling, has been referred to the Social Services system*
5   *numerous times. In a session with yet another therapist, Angela*
6   *is finally able to confront her childhood demons.*

7

8   I was named after an angel. Not a specific angel ... but
9   my father always thought I looked like an angel. That's what
10 he told me the day he found me home alone and ... *(Pause.)*
11 I was eleven. I had just started my period. I had blood all
12 over me. My mother never talked of such things. My mother
13 mostly didn't talk. She let Dad talk. Oh, he was quite the
14 talker. He cuddled me, called me his wounded angel, and
15 kissed ... he kissed ... *(She stops for a moment.)* where the
16 blood was. I asked him to call a doctor. He told me I didn't
17 need one. He said I only needed him, because he named me.
18   That's when I started to cry. And then he said he'd
19 wash the blood away. Told me I was bleeding because that's
20 what angels do who come to earth to sin. I said I never did,
21 but he said I must have or I wouldn't be like those other
22 women. I asked him if Mom bled. He just smiled. He smiled
23 as I started to fight him and as he hit me ... and then as he
24 pushed me down on the bed.
25   Oh God, there was so much blood. So much pain. I
26 never knew it could be so ... *(She begins to cry.)* My teacher
27 at school noticed something. I don't know what. I tried to
28 hide everything. My Dad was a nice guy most of the time.
29 But not in naming. Now I live somewhere else where the

1   man doesn't talk to me and the woman fusses over me. It's
2   weird. There are moments when I want to go home. There are
3   moments when I never want to see my Dad again.
4   I know one thing. When I get some money, I'm going to
5   change my name.
6
7
8
9
10
11
12
13
14
15
16
17
18
19
20
21
22
23
24
25
26
27
28
29
30
31
32
33
34
35

Files
by Amy Bryan

1   Amy   Young Adult/Adult

2

3   *Amy, a young office clerk, has very interesting work habits.*
4   *Sitting at her office desk surrounded by stacks of files and a bottle*
5   *of alcohol, she looks inside each file, closes it, and then throws*
6   *it over her shoulder.*

7

8   **Seven dollars an hour. That's it! Seven bucks an hour**
9   **to sit here and go through all this. Files. Files everywhere!**
10   **I can't even see over my desk most of the time. It is**
11   **ridiculous. I will let you in on a little secret. I don't know**
12   **what any of it means. They tell me to file them, so I do. If**
13   **they happen to ask me about any information in them, I**
14   **just tell them I'm busy.** *(She opens a file and studies it.)* **They**
15   **have names and numbers in them. They have got to be**
16   **important, right? I mean they hired me to do this! But the**
17   **terrible truth is I have absolutely no idea what I'm doing.**
18   **Shh! Don't tell the boss. To be quite honest with you, I am**
19   **not even sure what we do here. 'What do you do for a living?'**
20   **I am often asked. I reply with 'I work for a company.' Then**
21   **they ask the killer, 'What kind of company?'** *(In a questioning*
22   *tone.)* **'A big one?' That's usually the end of the**
23   **conversation, and my dignity.**
24   **I will let you in on a little secret. Every single file does**
25   **not need to be put in its place.** *(She takes a large gulp from*
26   *the bottle.)* **Not at all!** *(She drinks again, now apparently very*
27   *drunk.)* **Who needs order!** *(She drinks again and then holds the*
28   *bottle out in front of her to the audience.)* **Hey, do you want**
29   **some?** *(She quickly pulls the bottle back.)* **Well, you can't have**

1   it! I'm the one doing all the work. You lazy ... *(She cuts herself*
2   *off, changing the subject.)* You know sometimes I think those
3   files are out to get me. Yes sir, they just sit there all quiet, but
4   sometimes I wonder if they are really up to something.
5   *(Holding back laughter.)* Well, I guess I should get back to work!
6   *(She bursts into laughter and drops her bottle on top of one of the*
7   *files, soaking it.)*
8   Oh no! Not that file! That file is terribly important for
9   something. *(She takes a handkerchief from her desk and begins to*
10 *clean off the file.)* This isn't working. *(She holds the file over her*
11 *mouth and shakes it. She then brings the file to her mouth and then*
12 *proceeds to lick it clean.)* This is not helping! I have got to use
13 my head. That's it. *(She begins to rub the file on her head,*
14 *desperate to clean it.)* How can I save this file? *(She looks at the*
15 *audience.)* Does anyone out there know CPR? *(She removes the*
16 *papers from the file and wrings them out over the bottle, as the*
17 *phone on her desk rings.)* Come in! *(The phone rings again.)* Oh!
18 It's the phone. *(She picks up the phone and speaks into the*
19 *receiver.)* It's only the phone. *(She goes back to wringing out the*
20 *papers as the phone rings once again. As she picks it up, she talks*
21 *into the wrong end of the phone.)* Hello? I'm sorry, I can't hear
22 you. Oh! *(She realizes her mistake and turns the phone around.)*
23 Hello? Hello, Allan. *(She looks at the audience.)* Ssh! It's the
24 boss. *(Into the phone.)* Yes? Which file? The Kroeger file?
25 Certainly you can pick it up. No everything is fine, the files are
26 almost done. *(She looks around at the countless files surrounding*
27 *her.)* Yes sir, everything is fine. Nothing is wrong.
28   I am not in the dark on the procedure, or taking too many
29 breaks ... *(Suddenly.)* ... or doing anything illegal like drinking
30 on the job and destroying files. I am positive sir. Yes, I am
31 aware of how important the files are. *(She shrugs to the*
32 *audience as if to say she doesn't really know.)* Yes sir, right away.
33 *(She hangs up the phone.)* He is coming to pick up the Kroeger
34 file. *(She looks through a few of the files, then notices the paper she*
35 *has ruined in her hand is the Kroeger file.)* No! What am I going

1   **to do?** *(There is a knock at the door. She shoves the papers down*
2   *her shirt and opens the door.)* **I'm busy!** *(She slams the door*
3   *closed.)* **Now back to work.** *(She sits at her desk, putting her feet*
4   *up on the desk. She gets another bottle from her desk.)* **I love files.**
5
6
7
8
9
10
11
12
13
14
15
16
17
18
19
20
21
22
23
24
25
26
27
28
29
30
31
32
33
34
35

Mae

by Susan Pomerance

1 Mae   Teen/Young Adult

2

3 *Mae is an insecure young lady with unmistakable notions about*
4 *romance and adventure. Her prospects for a promising romantic*
5 *adventure, however, are dashed by an unlikely incident and*
6 *some humorous antics at a Barnes & Noble bookstore.*

7

8   I ran into him at Barnes & Noble. He didn't say, 'Hi,'
9 'Hello,' 'How are you,' 'Nice day,' nothing like this. The first
10 thing he says to me, right out of the blue, is, 'You're born,
11 you struggle, and then you die.' *(Beat.)* Right. He actually
12 said this. Is this off-the-wall, or what? *(Beat.)* I know, you
13 just don't hear opening lines like this every day. He was
14 totally different from anyone I've ever met. And he was
15 different looking, too. Had this real intense stare and hair
16 that looked like it'd been cut with hedge trimmers. And, oh
17 yeah, he had a goatee. How many guys do you know with a
18 goatee? *(Beat.)* Right, not any. And he was wearing this
19 beat-up old corduroy jacket and a pair of wire-rimmed
20 glasses with one of the stems held on with a straight pin.
21 He was strange, totally different. And not bad looking. He
22 was kinda handsome, actually.
23   Anyway, here I was, browsing through the magazines,
24 checking out the fan mags, when he walks up carrying
25 seven tons of poetry. He wanted to know if I'd ever read *On*
26 *the Road.* When I asked him if it was published by the Auto
27 Club, he got this funny look around the mouth like he's just
28 swallowed Liquid Plumber. Hey, I was serious. Then he
29 asked me if I'd ever read *War and Peace.* When I said why

1 would I want to waste my time reading it when I could rent the
2 video, he got this funny look again.
3   Then he asked me if I'd like to have lunch, and I accepted.
4 Ordinarily, I'd never do anything like this, but this dude was
5 so different, I just couldn't resist. So we go to this health-food
6 place, The Raging Lettuce, over on Fourth Street. Of course,
7 he's a strict vegetarian, so he orders up this concoction made
8 up of carrots and spinach and seaweed and junk that they
9 grind up in a blender. When they pour it out, it looks like
10 gremlin barf. There wasn't a cheeseburger in sight, so I
11 ordered a salad that looked and tasted like hay. Awful.
12   During lunch, he goes on and on about Shakespeare and
13 Yates and Dylan Thomas. His name was Dylan, by the way.
14 Figures, right? And the only films he liked were foreign. He
15 loved subtitles. Said they were pure. When I asked him how
16 he could read the subtitles and watch the picture at the same
17 time, he didn't have an answer. When the waitress brought
18 the check, he said to her, 'You're born, you struggle, and then
19 you die.' This is when I excused myself to go to the ladies'
20 room. Instead, I left the poet with his vomit milkshake.
21   I'm staying out of Barnes & Noble.
22
23
24
25
26
27
28
29
30
31
32
33
34
35

Why I Want to Be
Your Junior Asia Miss
by Lauren D. Yee

1 Bekki Lee Kim   Teen/Young Adult
2
3 *Bekki Lee Kim, a young Asian woman, is a contestant for the*
4 *Junior Asia Miss scholarship competition. Although attractive*
5 *and perky, Bekki Lee doesn't appear very poised in the question-*
6 *and-answer part of the contest.*
7
8   Hi, there. My name is Bekki Lee Kim and I want to be
9 your next Junior Asia Miss! And remember, that's spelled
10 B-E-K-K-I with a 'T' and two 'K's.' *(Making horrible pun.)*
11 'Cause I want to be your next Junior Asia Miss, O-Kay?
12 *(Waits for audience laughter — not surprisingly, there is none.)* All
13 right, then! So I guess now is the time when I read the
14 questions. All right, super! *(Looks left, then right for question*
15 *cards and realizes she has them in her hands. Giggles.)* Well,
16 here they are! All right.
17   'Why do you want to be the next Junior Asia Miss?'
18 Why? Like a reason? Well ... umm ... err ... I do have a
19 reason. There's always a reason, but ... can we get back to
20 that? Wait! *(Takes out a piece of paper from bra and reads*
21 *woodenly.)* Because I believe that Asia is a really special
22 place and it has many people. *(Smiles, puts paper away.)*
23 Take China for instance. It's a very special state. And it's
24 very ... *(Takes out a second paper, reads, pronounces word*
25 *incorrectly.)* 'de-ver-se.' Like in Hong Kong. Everybody in
26 Hong Kong pretends to be British. Have you ever noticed
27 that? I mean, come on! Stop playing with me. I know you're

1   not Englishmen. And speaking of Englishmen, I've always
2   wondered: If we call people from England, Englishmen and
3   people from France, Frenchmen ... why aren't there
4   Japanmen? Or Chinamen? Therefore, if you make me Junior
5   Asia Miss, I pledge to do my best to equalize the system and
6   make sure 'Chinaman' is used as often as possible.

7   'What does being Asian mean to you?' Well, being Asian
8   means a lot to me. Like it's absolutely who I am. Other than
9   being young and female, I think being Asian is sooo much a
10 part of me. Peace out to the mother country! *(Makes peace*
11 *signs to the camera.)* All right then. On to the next one.

12 'What would you do if you became the next Junior Asia
13 Miss?' Do? You mean, who would I do? *(Waits for instructions,*
14 *then glances down at paper.)* Oh, I'm sorry. *(Giggles.)* There's
15 more. 'How would you be a positive role model for young girls?'
16 A model? Well, yes, I would love to be a model! I think it's very
17 important that if you're a model, you be a positive one, too.
18 Actually, any kind of model would be fine with me. Shoe
19 modeling, hair model, hand modeling. *(Voice of person in*
20 *audience, 'It's role model, stupid!')*

21 A ... what model? Ohhh, that kind of role model. *(Pause,*
22 *shocked.)* What's so funny? Why are you laughing? *(Realizes.)*
23 Okay, so I'm not a genius. I've never done calculus. I can't
24 explain Kepler's laws for all the tea in China. I don't even know
25 how much tea is 'all the tea in China!' I'm no Edgar Einstein,
26 but I think it's unfair of you to assume that I'm here just
27 because I'm young and beautiful and the ugly girls aren't
28 because they're young and ugly. Because this scholarship
29 competition is not about looks — it's about — it's about —
30 well, it's not about looks!

31 It's about being Asian. And about being proud of it and
32 doing something positive. And you don't have to do quantum
33 physics or quote Webster's Dictionary to do any of that. I may
34 not know ... *(Pronouncing the following subjects incorrectly.)*
35 chem — mistry or psy — koology or physo — lolerogy, but I

1 think that whatever I do does a whole lot more than those
2 smart people who know everything and do nothing. That's why
3 I think I should be Junior Asia Miss — because I'll try. And
4 that's what makes Asia a very special country. *(Triumphant*
5 *and about to exit, she trips on her skirt.)*
6
7
8
9
10
11
12
13
14
15
16
17
18
19
20
21
22
23
24
25
26
27
28
29
30
31
32
33
34
35

Ho Ho Ho, Done Done Done, Mom in Love

by Barbara Lindsay

1 Candy, Tricia, and Amber   Teens/Young Adults
2
3 *Here is a 3 x 3 offering of monologs that chronicle adolescent and*
4 *young adult characters engaged in mishaps and missteps in*
5 *dealing with Christmas Eve confrontations, New Year's Eve*
6 *resolutions, crushes, and infatuations.*
7
8   **Ho Ho Ho**
9   *(CANDY enters hesitantly, and walks slowly Center Stage.*
10 *She has decided to tell her cheerful sister-in-law the awful truth:*
11 *Christmas is hateful and depressing, and she is secretly*
12 *convinced that everyone else thinks so, too.)*
13   **Of course I'm depressed. It's Christmas. Christmas is**
14 **depressing. Name me one person who doesn't think**
15 **Christmas is depressing. I'll bet even Norman Rockwell**
16 **hated Christmas. I'll bet he hated everything he ever**
17 **painted, all cute and adorable and home sweet home,**
18 **everybody making nice and goofy with love. When was it**
19 **ever like that? Name me one Christmas that didn't have a**
20 **fight in it, or some present that you gave somebody that you**
21 **knew they hated, only they had to act like they loved it, but**
22 **they knew you knew they didn't so you both got depressed.**
23 **I mean, fruitcake, for heaven's sake. Everybody hates**
24 **fruitcake, but we go on baking them and giving them to**
25 **people we don't want to buy real presents for, year after**
26 **year, like this big conspiracy of misery that for some reason**
27 **we all agree to pretend not to notice. It's awful. It's**

1 depressing. You take Santa Claus away and all you got left is
2 fruitcake and shopping and the tree dropping needles all over
3 the carpet. I miss Santa Claus. I do. When you believe in
4 Santa, there's a point to it all. Once that's gone, it's just
5 empty and exhausting. Why hide the eggs if there's no Easter
6 Bunny? If there's no Tooth Fairy, what does losing a tooth
7 mean, except that you're getting older and starting to decay
8 and someday you're going to die. That's all any of it is, just a
9 picture we paint so we don't have to think about the fact that
10 even if we're happy and have a great life, we're still going to
11 rot and die and rot some more. You think I'm in bad shape
12 now, just wait for New Year's Eve!
13
14   Done Done Done
15   *(TRICIA rushes on stage waving a fistful of well-worn sheets of*
16 *paper. She announces to her friends that she has finally fulfilled her*
17 *New Year's Eve resolution: to complete several years' worth of left*
18 *over 'To Do' lists.)*
19   I DID IT! *(She dances and jumps ecstatically.)* I did it. I have
20 finished every item on every 'To Do' list! *Every one.* I'm done.
21 *(She dances and howls.)* Everything. *(She reads off various lists.)*
22 Sew buttons on blouse. Check. Go skydiving. Check. Scrub
23 behind stove. Check. Once in a lifetime is enough for that
24 chore, believe me. Learn Spanish. Si. Answer every letter,
25 e-mail, and phone call. Check. I know there'll be more, but I'm
26 caught up is the point. Buy new lampshade. Check. Hem
27 tartan skirt. Check. Well, I threw it away. Didn't fit any more.
28 You see, you see? That's the beauty of being caught up now.
29 I can hem the skirts *while they still fit.*
30   See *Citizen Kane.* Check, finally. Replace toilet paper
31 holder, check. Clean out garage, have garage sale, check
32 check. *Start working out twice a week.* Check, and I look
33 great, thank you very much. Meet Mick Jagger. Okay, now
34 this, this is a story all by itself, so don't get me started, but
35 yes, indeed, check. Empty cupboards, wipe shelves, check,

1 balance checkbook, check, throw New Year's party, check. I
2 mean everything. Everything. It's all checked. Chores,
3 errands, projects, call, see, fix, start, clean, buy, have, do, be.
4 Done. I'm done!
5   You have no idea, no idea what this feels like. All my life
6 has been spent scrambling to get caught up, and always this
7 avalanche of 'to do to do to do.' This moment is like the
8 beginning of life. I'm done. There is no more 'someday' for me.
9 It's all — right now. *(Pause.)* Okay, there is one thing I didn't
10 do, but it's not something I can really do on my own, so it
11 doesn't count, and everything else is ... done. *(Pause.)* I mean,
12 I didn't write it down. It's so 'someday,' it could just never
13 happen at all, so I can't wait around for that before my life
14 begins. So my life begins here. Right here, right now. In this
15 moment. *(Pause.)*
16   I think I put it on one list early on. *(Looks through lists.)* Oh
17 yeah, yeah, here it is. 'Get married.' Yeah, right. Like that's
18 something you just do, like sewing on buttons. Right. *(She*
19 *tears up that one list.)* Hey, anybody can get married. I met Mick
20 Jagger. So. *(She tosses the pieces into the air.)* What the heck.
21 *(She tosses all the lists into the air.)* I feel so free. The future is
22 standing open before me, like a huge, blank, empty canvas. I
23 can do anything now. Anything. *(Pause.)* Anything I want.
24 *(Pause.)* Whatever life throws, I can catch it and deal with it on
25 the spot. *(Pause.)* So come on, Life. I'm ready. *(Pause.)* Ready
26 for anything. *(Pause.)* Anything at all.
27
28   Mom in Love
29   *(AMBER, a teenager, talks to her best friend about a serious*
30 *problem at home. Her divorced mother has fallen in love and is*
31 *wrapped up in her own romantic affairs. To AMBER, this is all just*
32 *too 'yucky' to bear!)*
33   Okay, so, like, you know, he's all, 'Blah blah blah,' and
34 she's all, 'Quack quack quack' and I'm all, like 'Okay, so,
35 whatever.' I mean, you know, like yuck. Like, it's all, like you

1 know, ghoulish and everything. I mean, like, it all makes all
2 this whole love thing, you know, really, like, suspect. I mean,
3 you know, she's, like, my mom. It's creepy. I mean, yuck. I
4 mean, she's got this, like, smile now that just makes me want
5 to barf. 'La la la la, sing sing, snicker snicker.' *My mom.* I
6 can't, like, go to her now and ask her stuff or tell her anything.
7 She's all, like, practically licking her chops and winking. It's
8 just too weird. I don't have anybody who's, like, you know,
9 normal I can go to and say, like, 'I met this guy,' 'cause she's
10 all, like, 'Oh me too, me too.' My stuff is all, like, nothing,
11 'cause she's all, you know, filled up with her stuff now and it's
12 disgusting. I don't even want to sleep at the house any more.
13 I mean, *my mom.* It's not even fun to talk about how she's all,
14 like, you know, the noises she makes or whatever. I mean,
15 yuck. I mean, where is she? I just thought it would be so cool
16 to have, like, some quiet old guy come in and read the paper
17 and, like, watch TV and support us and everything. But this
18 is so not cool, this is, like, dude, this sucks. Like, it's *my*
19 time, you know? It's not her time. She's, like, middle-aged.
20 She's got these, like, fat bags above her elbows and she's all,
21 you know, she's my mom. I just don't even have a remote how
22 to handle this. I keep, like, you know, feeling all homesick and
23 everything. Only I'm already home.
24
25
26
27
28
29
30
31
32
33
34
35

My Parents
by Joe McCabe

1 Daughter   Teen/Young Adult

2

3   *Here is an inventive comic monolog that relies on a sly turn of*
4   *words and a cascade of familiar phrases, quotations, and cliches*
5   *to sketch a deliciously funny portrait of parents as seen through*
6   *the eyes of their children.*

7

8   When Mom first met him, Dad was a diamond in the
9   rough with a gift of gab, a man of the world and a man of his
10 word, and a barrel of laughs who never missed a trick. His
11 big heart was in the right place, and he had an open mind
12 on most subjects. Mom had a mind of her own and a
13 memory like an elephant. She wasn't born yesterday, and
14 she had a good head on her shoulders, but she was a
15 backseat driver who made mountains out of molehills. She
16 looked every gift horse in the mouth. Dad always had the
17 courage of his convictions, but sometimes he seemed scared
18 to death of her, even though her bark was worse than her
19 bite. Money burned a hole in his pocket, but year in, year
20 out, Mom saved all she could for the rainy days to come.
21 Sometimes he'd put all his eggs in one basket or count his
22 chickens before they hatched, and when he had egg on his
23 face she expected him to eat crow. She'd cry over spilled
24 milk, and she'd beat a dead horse till she was blue in the
25 face. He'd bite his tongue and swallow his pride. He'd bend
26 over backwards for her, but he rarely let her get him down.
27 He'd go the extra mile and look for the silver lining along the
28 way. She never quite put him in his place. Mom tried to put
29 the best face on things, and Dad usually played along with

her. 'We Could Make Believe,' from *Showboat*, was Their Song. They knew how to make a virtue of necessity; they stuck together through thick and thin; they made the best of their hard bargain. Dad was generous. Mom was fair. If it weren't for them, I wouldn't be here at all. If it weren't for their nurturing, I wouldn't be the way I am. Between them they taught me to keep a straight face and a civil tongue, to keep my eyes open and my nose clean, to keep my shirt on and my fingers crossed. They told me to give life my best shot, to roll with the punches, to live and learn. Mom wanted to have the last word. Dad preferred to have the last laugh.

Dinner For ?
by Molly G. Schuchat

1 Penny   Adult

2

3   *Penny, a mature female executive, reclines in a therapist's chair*
4   *clutching a box of Kleenex. She is obviously distraught as she*
5   *tries to cope with her pent-up emotions. From time to time, Penny*
6   *rises to act out parts of her story for the therapist.*

7

8   Why am I here, Doctor? I need to know if Steve loves me
9   or hates me. I thought maybe you could figure it out. That's
10 my problem. What I mean is — I better tell you the
11 background.
12   I rushed in from work to pick up the phone before they
13 hung up and it was Steve. At his most persuasive and
14 proud: 'I've got these clients here who love good home
15 cooking, three of them, and we'll be there in half an hour.
16 Love ya.' And he hangs up. It wasn't the first time in our
17 three year marriage that he has done this to me. It's a
18 challenge, and I won it hands down the first time, so he
19 keeps upping the stakes. But I'm not thinking about that.
20 I'm rushing to the refrigerator and the pantry shelf and
21 trying to decide whether to work on a main dish first or to
22 fix dips to keep them drinking while I have more time for
23 fixing dinner in the kitchen.
24   That first time we'd been married three — is everything in
25 threes? — weeks, it was his mother. 'Hello, darling. Mother's
26 in town for the day and I want to bring her home, not have
27 her take us out for dinner. O.K.?' What could I say? I would
28 do anything for his mother, because he was so wonderful and
29 she raised him. 'So we'll be there in an hour.' I knew I could

1   handle that. I made a sardine spread for drinks — Steve sees
2   that we're well stocked with beer and wine and other stuff. Then
3   I took the leftover chicken, frozen vegetables, onions, etc. and
4   made a pie crust cover. I used a fork to make some pretty
5   designs in the cover, too. Presentation is everything. Almost.
6   Then I put these darling pot pies in the oven.
7   So, not having any flowers for the table, I took some raw
8   vegetables and did them up in a bouquet and put little candles
9   around them. Pretty! Dessert was canned fruit, mixed up with
10   some lemon added — I do keep things in the house, did even
11   when I was just a brand-new bride and even before that when
12   I was single. Anyway, my mother-in-law was thrilled — with
13   the vegetable centerpiece — and enjoyed dinner and
14   everything. She was a peach! Steve was really proud of me
15   and bragging to his mother about his capable little bride.
16   That's what I thought then ... this latest incident.
17   I'm running back and forth trying to decide and time is
18   ticking away. I can hear it! I have a wonderful lasagna in the
19   freezer, but it will take an hour and a half — well, we'll drink
20   it up. So I put that in the oven and concentrated on the hors
21   d'oevres. Fortunately, I have some cottage cheese, so I mix
22   that with the other stuff, which I have, including the capers,
23   to make liptaur cheese — it's very low cholesterol, actually,
24   and there's one at least of the clients who is concerned with
25   his heart. Steve's too young, and he's very fit anyway and
26   does take good care. A salad? I didn't have any lettuce but I
27   had lots of cucumbers for some reason so I chopped those up
28   with onions and olives. Keep their teeth in condition with the
29   chewing. No Italian bread, but I can make garlic bread out of
30   just about anything, So I started to do that with some white
31   bread, which I cut thick, from the freezer. And I had parmesan
32   cheese as well as garlic, so that was working out.
33   Now — into the dining area with ten minutes to go, thank
34   goodness the mats are clean and I have some clean napkins,
35   too. And candles. No flowers — maybe one of them will bring

1 some? Probably not. I'll try what I did with my mother-in-law that
2 time. Do you know, in all this rushing around I forgot to take off
3 my coat? So I rush to the hall closet and the phone rings. So I
4 rush back with one sleeve on and one sleeve off and — it's
5 Steve. 'Honey,' he says, all sweetness. 'Honey.' God, he's going
6 to bring more men and there isn't enough lasagna. 'Honey, we
7 decided it would be too much work for you, so come and meet
8 us at the Greek Place. Ten minutes?' And he hangs up.
9   And I sat down on the floor, one sleeve in and one sleeve
10 out, and cried. Is he showing me off, or trying to drive me nuts?
11
12
13
14
15
16
17
18
19
20
21
22
23
24
25
26
27
28
29
30
31
32
33
34
35

The Mystery of Trees
by Laura Zam

1 Maggie   Teen/Young Adult
2
3 *Maggie, a sensitive young woman who likes to wear Indian*
4 *jewelry and skirts, is a forlorn, solitary figure surrounded by a*
5 *mystical aura. Here, she interprets her "visions" to an*
6 *unsuspecting man who has recently become her boyfriend.*
7
8   Trees frighten me. They know things, and I don't like it.
9 I also know things — hey, I'm natural. But I don't know
10 what the trees know. Sometimes, I pretend I'm a tree to see
11 if I can access the same information. I stretch myself up,
12 up, up ... I bet you didn't know it but I'm a visionary! I've
13 been having visions since I was four. The first vision I ever
14 had was of my grandfather beating me up, beating me up,
15 beating me up. And then the next morning, he was dead. I
16 see things. The thing is, I don't see what the trees see, and
17 that's why I need your help.
18   I once asked the trees for help. I went to a dense forest
19 in Maine and pleaded with the trees to impart some of their
20 wisdom. Then, just as I got to the end of the forest, I stepped
21 on some wet leaves and had a blinding vision. It was a vision
22 of me, holding a tree branch and swinging it around and
23 around and around. In that moment, I understood the
24 meaning of life. Completely. It was a gender thing: Male and
25 Female inherent in all things on the planet — organic and
26 inorganic. Or something like that ... It's so hard to put into
27 words. But it was everything, and I was so grateful for this
28 insight. Slowly, I turned around to thank the trees for, you
29 know, helping me. But when I looked at them, they were

1 laughing. 'You've got it all wrong,' they rustled. And then they
2 mocked me with their ... height.
3   About a week later I had an ecstatic vision of the Amazon
4 Rain Forest being bulldozed as people all over the world
5 rejoiced by sitting at long mahogany tables smoking their
6 lungs out. The thing is, everyone at these tables was
7 extremely brilliant and funny. And then it struck me: If we
8 could just get rid of all the trees in the world, everyone would
9 become more intelligent. Don't you get it? Trees intercept
10 knowledge. Why do you think people in cities know more? And
11 do you think it's an accident that we use paper to write?
12 You've got to help me. People in this world are stupid. Really,
13 really stupid! It's not just me. We all need more intelligence!
14 You've got to help me chop down all these trees — Because ...
15 the thing is, lately, I've been having a transcendent vision of a
16 cold, dark, rainy night.
17   I'm standing out in a treeless field and letting the lightning
18 touch me. See, this way there's nothing coming between me
19 and the light — a sharp, white light cutting through the black
20 infinity and impaling me with truth. And then I'll be dead. If
21 you don't help me, I think I'll be dead. The visions are coming
22 fast now ... Every minute ... Everyday ... Every minute. I told
23 you: I'm a visionary! Which is fine. Maybe it's O.K. to die while
24 being struck down by truth. Because, let's face it, the truth
25 always, always hurts.
26
27
28
29
30
31
32
33
34
35

Santa's Coming
by Les Marcott

1 Mall Elf   Teen/Young Adult
2
3 *In this light-hearted sketch, an exasperated mall "elf" tries to*
4 *explain the chronic tardiness of Santa Claus to a group of anxious*
5 *and restless children. The elf is apologetic, but perhaps a little too*
6 *brutal in Santa's defense!*
7
8   Gosh, kids, Santa's running a little late today. You
9 might even say he's been a little under the weather. He's
10 had a uh, uh ... stomach virus. Yeah, that's it, a stomach
11 virus. Ha. *(Beat.)* Okay, kids, gather round 'cause I've got a
12 big secret to tell you. *(Beat.)* You know, I can't lie to you.
13 Santa wants us to be truthful, right? Well, his tummy does
14 hurt along with his head but it's because of something we
15 adults call a hangover. Can you say that? Hangover. But
16 don't worry your little heads about it, 'cause it'll go away
17 soon. That's what we adults call a little hair of the dog.
18 Now, if you want to learn more about hangovers and other
19 alcohol related subjects you'll need to talk to your parents.
20   Not now. Later. Right now we need to get ready 'cause
21 *(Calling to the back.)* **SANTA WILL BE OUT HERE ANY**
22 **MINUTE.** *(Smiles to kids.)* Now, because Santa hasn't been
23 feeling so good, it's really important you keep your requests
24 really brief. You know what brief means? It means really
25 short. It means you ask for one thing only. Can you do that?
26 Can you ask for only one thing? Because if you take too
27 long, Santa might get really sick again and you don't want
28 that. So tell him what you want — that really special ONE
29 gift — then grab your candy cane, exit right and get the hell

1   out. *(Beat.)* Did I say that? Bad elf. Don't tell your parents I
2   said that 'cause then there might be an investigation of
3   Santa's Workshop and you really don't want that. Right?
4   Have you ever been in a restaurant during an INS raid? It
5   might be funny to look at but it's not funny for the elves. You
6   don't want the elves put on a bus and sent away do you? Elves
7   are good. They make things almost for free so Santa can
8   afford to give them to you. Aren't elves magical? Let's see if
9   we can't make some more magic and have Santa appear.
10   *(Calls out.)* **SANTA, WE'RE WAITING FOR YOU!** *(Back to kids.)*
11   He'll be out here any minute. And don't worry about Santa's
12   big black eye. He was so happy, he was kissing all the
13   mommies around the Christmas tree last night and one of the
14   daddies didn't understand. It was very exciting. Santa and
15   that daddy had a big long conversation and Santa accidentally
16   fell down. On his eye. But he's better now. None of you kids
17   have the last name of Holland, do you? Oh, good, just
18   checking. *(Looks over.)* Oh, my gosh, look kids! **IT'S SANTA!**
19   Okay, everybody, stay in line. Everyone gets a turn. Have a
20   Merry Christmas!
21
22
23
24
25
26
27
28
29
30
31
32
33
34
35

Torsal Communication
by Ken Friedman

1 Instructor   Adult
2
3 *An animated and hyperactive instructor provides a good-humored*
4 *examination of male-female relationships. She is an imposing*
5 *figure who holds her attentive students spellbound with her*
6 *classroom antics.*
7
8   Okay, ladies, you paid for the class. Now, did you get your
9 money's worth? You bet! Quick review! 'Relationships.' On
10 what are most male-female relationships based? Miss Clark?
11 Lust! Good. And how do we signal our lusty intentions? Miss
12 Lacey? Yes! 'B.L.' Body Language. Otherwise, known as 'T.C.'
13 Torsal Communication. Students, never underestimate what
14 you can do with your bod when your bod knows just what to
15 do. It's more than the tongue that speaketh. Quickly, gals,
16 name the three most important elements in your FBV:
17 Female Bodily Vocabulary. Pelvis, eyeballs and elbows! Did I
18 hear ears? Wake up. Ears are for later! For a man? It's his
19 knowing nod, his leer and his lip. For both sexes? Nostrils!
20 Excellent! And of course, gals, in an emergency, we have the
21 advantage ... our rear-end. Thrust it or bust it! *(Wiggling her*
22 *behind.)* Is it Esperanto? No! I call it Ass-peranto. Thank you.
23   Okay, you're at a party with Mr. Wrong, but in walks Mr.
24 Right. Now, we know the woman never makes the first
25 move unless he's famous or can get you a job, but with
26 what you've learned today, you can start a relationship
27 without even leaving your chair. How? Body Bingo! Pelvis,
28 eyeballs, elbows, and nostrils! Repeat: Pelvis, eyeballs,
29 elbows and nostrils. Everybody! Go! Unfurl the pearl!

1 *(Demonstrating.)* **Eyeballs angled, pelvis locked and loaded, left**
2 **elbow out, right nasal tuck, skirt above knee and the difficult**
3 **Norwegian knee nudge.** *(Flapping knees.)* **He's watching! Now,**
4 **free hand to waist, neck-torque; 30 degrees, hip-slip, knee**
5 **nudge, guy-glance. Good. Hold steady. This position is? 'The**
6 **Prelude to Passion.' Pretzel. Good. If blocked by a table, for**
7 **God's sakes, try to stand and go into the crucial eye-drift.**
8 **Eye-drift. Easy. Easy. Contact!**
9 **Now, a subtle breast heave. Good. Again. Ellen, heave.**
10 **Nice! Beverly, more nostril. Flare those babies! Good! Now,**
11 **reel him in. You've done it. Communication? Ladies, you have**
12 **just e-mailed his ass! His response? Look for the nod, the leer**
13 **and the lip. Two out of three and you'll meet in the kitchen.**
14 **Once there, touch his arm and that boy is yours! Thank you.**
15 **Next week, my award-winning seminar 'How to Break Up**
16 **Subconsciously.' Emphasizing the inverted elbow, facial hair**
17 **and timely drool. Read my book, no Xeroxing please, and tell**
18 **all your friends to buy it. Oh, and remember this, how do we**
19 **conceal our ignorance on most topics? By agreeing with**
20 **everything. I'm exhausted. Yes, you may stand and applaud.**
21 **Thank you. This was a great session. Thank you. Thank you.**
22 **I accept your ovation.**
23
24
25
26
27
28
29
30
31
32
33
34
35

Last Call
by Thomas W. Stephens

1 Woman   Young Adult/Adult
2
3 *An unidentified woman sits alone on a chair with a telephone*
4 *pressed to her ear, waiting for a pickup. There is an air of calmness*
5 *that surrounds her, but a foreboding sense of despair hovers*
6 *overhead. (The ellipses indicate pauses or moments of listening.)*
7
8   Hey-hey-hey, girlfriend. So, how's it going? ... Well, tell
9 me, it's such a long ... Oh, I know you've been ... Well, me
10 too, honey, you wouldn't believe, up to my ... Whoa, there's
11 all this catching up we ... Oh, yeah? Well, you are one hard
12 chick to get a hold of ... Right, I've tried you a couple ...
13 Actually, I've made quite a few ... Uh-huh ... And I didn't
14 care to, just, you know, leave another ... Message, who
15 knows, what if you were screening your calls and, well,
16 didn't ... Anyway, I mean ... Right, right ... So, anyway, I
17 am totally out-of-my-loving-head curious about ... Uh-huh,
18 well, him ... Who else, but, I mean the 'Hairball.' *(Laughs.)*
19   The horrendous, half-witted hairball ... Oh wow, he is such
20 a total ... Uh-huh, so what's ... You've been ... Oh, really? ...
21 No, no, no, he's still? — And he? — ... Oh, right — Actually, I
22 always thought ... When you, actually, you get down to it ...
23 oh, I know he is ... Right, if you overlook ... Uh-huh, those
24 qualities are the subtle ones, I know for a fact ... Well, and you
25 don't realize to start off with ... Gosh, that's so ... No! He
26 didn't! ... He — I mean, I mean, I mean, when? ... Talk about
27 Mr. Mover: he just — girl, I am on the floor ... And you didn't
28 call, you didn't let me ... I am seriously screaming here ...
29 Well, what's it look like? ... Oh man, I love platinum, I am

1 totally ... And it's ... Oh wow, an absolute boulder ... How can
2 you ... Whoa, your hand must be ... Uh-huh, dragging on the
3 terrazzo ... Serious-serious stuff, then ... So, when are you ...
4 When? I mean, that's ... I mean, it's like there's no time at all ...
5 There's no way you can ... You know, the gown, the invitations
6 and the ... Really? Oh, you have? ...
7   Well, mine never got to me, girlfriend, it never arrived —
8 but I've been having mail delivery problems ever since ... Oh,
9 uh-huh ... Is that a fact? ... No, no, I understand ... So, how
10 small, how intimate? ... Exactly, just ... How many people are
11 we talking here? ... I mean, I'm family, you know ... I said,
12 truth is, I am family too. In-laws are ... Well, if you're going to
13 go totally technical ... I am aware, technically speaking, that
14 Kenny is the in-law ... But then how many times have you said
15 to me, to my face, 'Your brother is such a hairball'? I mean,
16 you go, 'That Kenny ... ' Okay, deal is, you're right, you don't
17 use that word yourself, but still, the point, what the point
18 is ... I mean, I am the friend here. I'm the one who's always ...
19 It's me, I'm the only one ... No, I'm not upset, it's just that ...
20 I said, my feelings are not ... *(Tears start. She fights them back.*
21 *A beat.)*
22   No, I am not hurt ... Feelings have nothing to ... Why
23 would I ... No, no, of course not. I wish you could ... If you
24 could only take a look at me now, at this very minute, what a
25 smile you'd be ... How happy I am for ... It's just ... No, only
26 I ... I totally hate it when guys do this to us, to girlfriends, you
27 know ... I mean, they, they ... Well, they — totally interject
28 themselves, they intrude ... Yes, that's what I said intrude ...
29 Smack between us, like a slab of meat keeping apart the
30 bread in a sandwich ... No, I like him ... I do, I do, I'm, no
31 question, fond of ... Don't take me wrong, the fact is, what it
32 is is ... Oh wow, here's an idea. Oh honey, here's — why don't
33 I ... Uh-huh, what I want to do is ... I'm going to throw the
34 best party ever for you — that's right, you know, a shower ...
35 Well, you can have more than one, you can ... Oh — I know, I

1   know, I can imagine how busy ... Then, then, okay, when you
2   get back, then, when you ... Uh-huh, after Barbados ... Okay,
3   if that's what ... Oh, yeah, all right, we'll just wait and, and,
4   we can make plans to ... Oh, really? You do? Now? ... No,
5   seriously, that's not a problem ... Okay, uh-huh, bye for now,
6   then ... Right, we'll talk and talk and talk — who can stop
7   us? ... And girlfriend? ... Now, you be sure you have plenty of
8   pictures taken because I want to ... I just can't wait ... Bye,
9   then ... Uh-huh. Call me ... Bye. Bye ... *(She hangs up and turns*
10 *away.)*
11   **Freaking hairballs ...** *(She turns back to stare at the phone.)*
12
13
14
15
16
17
18
19
20
21
22
23
24
25
26
27
28
29
30
31
32
33
34
35

Marathon Runners
by Bob Ost

1 Two Runners   Young Adults/Adults
2
3 *The New York Marathon is the colorful backdrop for the following*
4 *"racy" monologs. Two young amateur women runners reflect on*
5 *the big race and provide an intimate glimpse of their personal*
6 *lives as they prepare to join the pack.*
7
8   **Mama Would Kill Me**
9
10   Mama would kill me if she knew I was out here in this
11 outfit, in full view of the immediate world. My mama doesn't
12 even approve of pants. The idea of gym clothes on a young
13 lady would just about give her apoplexy. And here we all
14 are, thousands upon thousands of us, running wild and free
15 on the streets of New York City in something that looks like
16 nothing more than fancy underwear!
17   Good thing there's a safe distance between mama and
18 me. Even for the small town I come from, mama is
19 considered a little ... conservative. Well, actually the word is
20 crazy. Totally overboard with the religion thing. Mama's
21 favorite decorating accent is the crucifix. There were so
22 many pictures of Jesus around, I thought it was my daddy
23 who deserted us. And she loves to light candles to keep
24 away the demons. Kind of like Carrie's mama, but with good
25 hair. Of course, I'm nothing like Carrie. No unusual powers
26 here. Heck, the only daggers I could send mama's way were
27 the looks I gave her before I left home. Since I moved to
28 New York, she's given me up as a lost soul. Doomed to hell.
29 But I don't let her bother me any more. *(She crosses herself.)*

1   Check out the shorts — aren't they adorable? I've got legs,
2   mama! And how about the matching headband and wrist
3   bands? An ensemble! I probably spent as much time picking
4   out the outfit as I did training for the race. Well, not really. But
5   don't you think this is a good look for me? You see, I've got
6   this kind of angular build, which really works in an athletic
7   context like the gym, or a marathon race. I mean, me in a
8   prom gown was pure disaster, but I actually fit right in here
9   with all these runners.

10   Have you seen some of them? All those really cool foreigners
11   who came over here from Nigeria and Sweden and who knows
12   where else to be in the New York Marathon. Like the United
13   Nations of Nike. And me from a small town in Delaware. Small
14   state, small town, small minds — it doesn't get much smaller
15   than that, does it? You know, there are more folks running this
16   race today than pass through my little town in a century.

17   What a crowd to get lost in! I got the biggest kick out of the
18   starting lineup at the Verrazano Bridge, more than a hundred
19   thousand runners psyched and raring to go, like wave after
20   wave of determined humanity. I like being lost in one of those
21   waves — this frantic rush of energy like the wildebeests in *The*
22   *Lion King* movies. And my mama would pass out to see me part
23   of the pack as sure as that little Simba's papa got trampled.

24   Yes, I know I'm just lollygaging, standing here talking to
25   you and lagging behind everyone. Heck, I haven't even made
26   up my mind if I'm going to bother to finish the race. That's not
27   important to me. I'm not a professional runner like a lot of the
28   others, I'm not going to break records or beat anyone's time.
29   I'm just here to do my personal best, which is pretty simple
30   since I've never actually run this thing before. So I'm already
31   doing my personal best. Right? Anyhow, that's what my
32   therapist says: I'm always doing my personal best. Well, at
33   least I'm living and breathing and part of something. Better
34   than sitting in my studio apartment staring at the walls and
35   waiting for the next doomsday call from mama.

1   Sandy Silverberg

2

3   Me run the marathon? The idea seemed totally out of

4   character. Well, ten years of jazz and modern isn't exactly

5   sitting on your rump, so I was in pretty good shape. But the

6   idea of training every day for this race? On top of the dance

7   classes, acting classes and endless open calls? And a survival

8   job at a midtown restaurant? I'm surprised my poor feet didn't

9   just get up and walk out on me as it was. Of course, they're

10 not a man — but that's another story.

11   Anyway, I get this showcase gig in an off-off-off Broadway

12 theatre. Well, actually it was in Brooklyn. Park Slope, if you

13 must know. Good part, questionable play, cute director. Real

14 cute. And at first I'm not going to even take it, but then I look

15 at my so-called resume and there's this big blank where the

16 last two years should be. Yeh, a big fat nothing is going on in

17 what is purported to be my theatre career, and mom is already

18 pressuring me to move back to Wisconsin. I figure I gotta do

19 something to justify calling myself an actress. Or it's back to

20 the cheese. In more ways than one.

21   So ... I'm second lead in 'The Bagel Diaries,' and I'm just

22 happy that it's only twelve performances because I know it's

23 a dead end. I mean, this play has about as much chance of

24 making it as that lazy drummer of a boyfriend who dumped me

25 last April. Know what they call a drummer without a

26 girlfriend? Homeless. It's the second to last performance, and

27 thank God the writer comes from a big family or else it would

28 have been pretty lonely up on that stage. But it's intermission,

29 and word spreads backstage that Sandy Silverberg is in the

30 audience. You know, the agent? Thank you, at last this play

31 has some meaning!

32   Well, I was good anyway. But I was great in the second act,

33 damn it. And let it go on the official record that Mr. Silverberg

34 noticed. And I get called in to his office the next week for an

35 interview. I mean, I could have peed, this stupid little

1 showcase in Park Slope actually gets me connected with one
2 of the top agents in the business.
3   So I do some major fluffing — hair, face, outfit ... and
4 resume. I fill in everything that needs to be filled in. Including
5 the last two years. And I am looking fabulous, and the resume
6 is looking ... believable. And I march into Silverberg's office, fill
7 out the paperwork his cute gay assistant hands me, and then
8 he calls me in. And we start to talk. And he asks me about
9 myself. And what I've done. And I'm searching the vacuum that
10 my brain has become for something, anything to impress this
11 man. Suddenly I see it: sitting on his desk, a framed shot of him
12 running the New York Marathon. And I say, 'Is that you?' And
13 he says proudly, 'Yep. I've run every year for the past four years.'
14 And without blinking an eye, I say, 'Me, too.'
15   Me too? Why didn't I just say I can build an atom bomb, or
16 remove my own appendix? Something easy. I don't know what
17 got into me, but there was no turning back. Sandy Silverberg
18 and I had the New York Marathon in common, and that is one
19 powerful bond. Like belonging to the same church. Which, by
20 the way, is no guarantee that the guy won't turn out to be a real
21 jerk — but that's another story. So Silverberg's office signed
22 me, and I found myself training for the damned marathon.
23   Six months of training. A few dance classes, and a lot
24 more running in Central Park. Sometimes with Sandy. And I
25 guess it's been worth it. He's sent me out for a few small
26 parts. I can finally write home and tell mom that I'm in a long
27 run in New York!
28
29
30
31
32
33
34
35

When They Speak of Rita
by Daisy Foote

1	Jeannie and Rita	Teen/Adult

2

3   *Duolog*

4   *This   duolog   for   two   women   conveys   a   sense   of*
5   *disillusionment and despair as Rita, a mature married woman*
6   *struggling to redefine herself after a failed affair, confides in*
7   *Jeannie, her son's seventeen-year-old girlfriend and mother of*
8   *his child. There are some awkward moments of tension as*
9   *the two characters share confidences and try to repair*
10   *damaged relationships. The ethical and moral exchanges of*
11   *dialog reveal inner conflicts, hidden desires, and frustrated*
12   *passions for both women. In playing the scene there should*
13   *be a sense of humility and dignity that allows each character*
14   *to achieve a measure of sympathy and understanding to*
15   *openly confront the complex issues raised in the confessional*
16   *conversation. There should also be a quiet strength in each*
17   *character that arouses our compassion.*

18

19   *Rita has recently returned home after a brief but intense*
20   *affair with Jimmy, a man much younger than herself. Life*
21   *with Asa, her husband of twenty years, has now become*
22   *more uncomfortable and tedious after her brief journey of*
23   *self-discovery.   Reflecting   on   her   past,   Rita   shares*
24   *troublesome thoughts with Jeannie, her son's girlfriend and*
25   *mother of his child.*

26

27 JEANNIE: I'm a good mother.
28 RITA: You know that already? Charlie's only a month old.
29 JEANNIE: When he was born, the minute they handed him

1   to me, I knew I was meant to be a mother.
2   RITA: As soon as they handed him to you —
3   JEANNIE: Yes.
4   RITA: And you think that will be enough?
5   JEANNIE: I think it will be more than enough.
6   RITA: It's not too late, you can still go to college.
7   JEANNIE: Rita —
8   RITA: You could go part-time, take some night courses.
9   JEANNIE: I don't want to.
10   RITA: But you were such a good student.
11   JEANNIE: I said I don't want to. And please stop trying to
12   make me feel bad about it.
13   RITA: I'm not.
14   JEANNIE: Oh yes you are. It's like you won't be happy until I
15   say to you, 'Rita, I've made a big mistake. I never should
16   have married Warren. I never should have had Charlie. You
17   were right all along.' I think you want me to be miserable.
18   RITA: That's not true.
19   JEANNIE: Then be happy for me, Rita. Be happy for me. *(A*
20   *beat.)* Why don't you go to college?
21   RITA: Oh be quiet.
22   JEANNIE: I'm serious. You're always telling everyone else to
23   go. You go.
24   RITA: I'm going to be forty-one next month.
25   JEANNIE: Oh that's so old.
26   RITA: I could never afford it. All we have is Asa's salary now.
27   I even tried to get a few of my cleaning jobs back. But
28   everyone has the same excuse, they've already hired
29   someone else.
30   JEANNIE: You were gone awhile.
31   RITA: That's not it. No one wants me around. I go to the
32   store to pick up some groceries or to the post office or
33   the dump, and everyone gets so quiet. I can feel their
34   eyes on me.
35   JEANNIE: It'll die down. Something else will happen, and

1   people will start talking about that.
2 RITA: But I don't know if people will forget. I think they have
3   the idea that I'm to blame for everything, not just me and
4   Jimmy running off but Jimmy's mother killing his father
5   and the California guy's wife —
6 JEANNIE: Now that's paranoid.
7 RITA: I'm the only one left. Everyone else is either dead, in
8   prison or moved away. People need someone to blame.
9 JEANNIE: And what about Jimmy? IF people are going to
10   blame you, then why not him too?
11 RITA: People feel sorry for him. He has to be a father and a
12   mother to the twins now. And people probably think I
13   made him run away with me, that he had no say in it. *(A*
14   *few beats.)* Is it true Jimmy's getting married?
15 JEANNIE: I heard something about it.
16 RITA: Who is she?
17 JEANNIE: Some girl he just met. I don't know anything
18   about her.
19 RITA: Well I'm glad he's found someone.
20 JEANNIE: Are you?
21 RITA: Yes I am.
22 JEANNIE: Sometimes I can't help but wonder.
23 RITA: About what?
24 JEANNIE: If you still don't miss him. *(A beat.)* Do you? *(A few*
25   *beats.)*
26 RITA: Right after I came back here, Jimmy came to see me.
27 JEANNIE: He came here, to this house?
28 RITA: Yes. He wanted me to move in with him and the twins.
29   He wanted me to marry him.
30 JEANNIE: Why did you do it, Rita? Why did you take off with
31   him? You and Asa have been married for twenty years.
32   You have a son. And no one, no one saw this coming. If
33   you were so unhappy, why didn't you tell someone?
34 RITA: No one would have heard me.
35 JEANNIE: How do you know that?

1   RITA: I'd get up in the morning, I'd put on the coffee. I'd make
2   breakfast. Then I'd go clean a couple of houses. I'd come
3   home, make Asa his lunch, clean our house. Then I'd start
4   supper, we'd watch some television. And if we were really
5   lucky, you or Jimmy would stop by. If not, we'd go to bed
6   and get up in the morning and start all over again. All that
7   sameness, I couldn't stand it any more.
8   JEANNIE: So you take off with Jimmy Reeves?
9   RITA: I'd give Jimmy something to eat, he would tell me that
10   I was the best cook in the world. I would tell him about
11   an idea and he would actually listen. He said I was a star,
12   a bright shining star.
13   JEANNIE: Oh, Rita.
14   RITA: You think I'm foolish.
15   JEANNIE: I just don't think you know how good you have it.
16   Asa is a good husband.
17   RITA: I'm here, aren't I? I'm cleaning his house and baking
18   his pies.
19   JEANNIE: If you really want something more than that, then
20   do something about it. *(Picking up the paper.)* If you don't
21   think school is possible, look in the employment section,
22   see if anything catches your eye.
23   RITA: I don't have any experience.
24   JEANNIE: Well maybe you should go back to that catering
25   place and tell them you'll take the job bussing tables.
26   RITA: Why would I want to do that?
27   JEANNIE: It's a place to start, Rita.
28   RITA: I couldn't.
29   JEANNIE: Why?
30   RITA: I just couldn't.
31   JEANNIE: Suit yourself.
32
33
34
35

Legal Acknowledgments

Copyright Caution

Copyright laws exist to protect the artistic and intellectual property rights of creators of original works. All creative works, such as scripts, are considered copyrighted. There are, however, a number of "fair use" exceptions for educational or instructional purposes related to classroom performance. The scripts in this volume are fully protected under the copyright laws of the United States, the British Empire, the Dominion of Canada, and all other countries of the Copyright Union. For additional information related to full-scale productions or other available scripts please contact the author or the author's agent at the address listed.

The Age of Innocence

Coming of Age

Memories of Viola by Jim Danek. Copyright © 2003 by Jim Danek. Reprinted by permission of the author. For additional information please contact the author at 3194 Portis, St. Louis, Missouri 63116 or at itchy1@mindspring.com.

The Princess of Rome, Ohio by Jonathan Joy. Copyright © 2003 by Jonathan Joy. Reprinted by permission of the author. For additional information please contact the author at joyjonathan@yahoo.com.

The Colors of Childhood by Tami Canaday. Copyright © 2004 by Tami Canaday. Reprinted by permission of the author. For additional information please contact the author at 6553 Welch Street, Arvada, Colorado 80004 or at evaeve@aol.com.

Yesterday Came Too Soon by Jamal Williams. Copyright © 2003 by Jamal Williams. Reprinted by permission of the author. For additional information please contact the author at 471 McDonough Avenue, Brooklyn, New York 11233 or at jamitt50@yahoo.com.

Mirrors Remembered by Cary Wong. Copyright © 2003 by Cary Wong. Reprinted by permission of the author. For additional information please contact the author at P. O. Box 20328, Columbus Circle Station, New York, New York 10023. *Mirrors Remembered* was commissioned by the Manhattan Theatre Club and produced by New York Stage and Film.

I Never Asked by Elyzabeth Gregory Wilder. Copyright © 2001 by Elyzabeth Gregory Wilder. Reprinted by permission of the author from *Hot Blooded New Monologues* by members of Youngblood (Playscripts.com 2001). For additional information please contact the author at ElyzabethW@aol.com.

The Woman Who Cooked Her Husband by Debbie Isitt. Copyright © 1991, 1993 by Debbie Isitt. First published in 1993 by Josef Weinberger, Ltd (pka Warner/Chappell Ltd). Reprinted by permission of Josef Weinberger, Ltd. For additional information please contact the publisher at Josef Weinberger, Ltd., 12-14 Mortimer Street, London W1T, 3JJ, England.

Romeo and Juliet, Part II by Sandra Hosking. Copyright © 1999 by Sandra Hosking. Reprinted by permission of the author. For additional information please contact the author at 5819 N. Vincent Road, Newman Lake, Washington 99025 or at sandrahosking@hotmail.com.

The Age of Rebellion

Junk by Melvin Burgess. Adapted for the stage by John Retallack. Copyright © 2003 by John Retallack. Reprinted by permission of the author and Methuen Publishing Limited. For additional information please contact the publisher at Methuen Publishing Limited, 215 Vauxhall Bridge Road, London SW1V, 1EJ England.

Dress Up by Erin Murtaugh. Copyright © 2001 by Erin Murtaugh. Reprinted by permission of the author from *Hot Blooded New Monologues* by members of Youngblood (Playscripts.com 2001). For additional information please contact the author at 7717 Romaine Street, West Hollywood, California 90046.

The General of Hot Desire by John Guare. Copyright © 1998 by John Guare. Reprinted by permission of the author from *Love's Fire* staged by The Acting Company of New York. For additional information please contact the author at 51 5th Avenue, Apartment 5 A, New York, New York 10003.

A Blue Streak by Staci Swedeen. Copyright © 2002 by Staci Swedeen. Reprinted by permission of the author. For additional information please contact the author at 130 New Broadway, Sleepy Hollow, New York 10591 or at staciswede@aol.com.

The Gilded Age

The Drunk Monologues by Diane F. Spodarek. Copyright © 2003 by Diane F. Spodarek. Reprinted by permission of the author. For additional information please contact the author at 385 Grand Street, # L 1508, New York, New York 10002 or at dianespodarek@aol.com.

Tough Cookies by Edward Crosby Wells. Copyright © 2001 by Edward Crosby Wells. Reprinted by permission of the author. For additional information please contact the author at edd@edwardcrosbywells.com.

Downsizing by Joseph Robinette. Copyright © 2003 by Joseph Robinette. Reprinted by permission of the author from *125 Original Audition Monologues*, Dramatic Publishing 2003. For additional information please contact the author at the Department of Theatre, Rowan University, Glassboro, New Jersey 08028 or at robinettej@rowan.edu.

Othello Undercover by Dave Tucker. Copyright © 2002 by Dave Tucker. Reprinted by permission of the author. For additional information please contact the author at P. O. Box 4032, Kent, Washington 98089 or at dave@davetucker.org.

Lemonade Lagoon by Christine Rusch. Copyright © 1997 by Christine Rusch. Reprinted by permission of the author. For additional information please contact the author at P. O. Box 202, Wyandotte, Michigan 48192 or at lsoperhaps@aol.com.

The Food Monologues by Kerri Kochanski. Copyright © 2003 by Kerri Kochanski. Reprinted by permission of the author. For additional information please contact the author at njdliterary@hotmail.com.

Curse of the Devil by Kent R. Brown. Copyright © 2003 by Kent R. Brown. Reprinted by permission of the author from *125 Original Audition Monologues,* Dramatic Publishing 2003. For additional information please contact the author at kentbrown@aol.com.

Cherchez Dave Robicheaux by Nina Lanai Wright. Copyright © 2002 by Nina Lanai Wright. Reprinted by permission of the author. For additional information please contact the author at lanai.wright@verizon.net.

Kitchen Sink Drama by Andrew Biss. Copyright © 2003 by Andrew Biss. Reprinted by permission of the author. For additional information please contact the author at andrewbiss@earthlink.net.

An American Daughter by Wendy Wasserstein. Copyright © 1998 by Wendy Wasserstein. Reprinted by permission of Harcourt Brace & Company. For additional information please contact the publisher at 6277 Sea Harbor Drive, Orlando, Florida 32887.

The Sphere Hunt by Nancy Gall-Clayton. Copyright © 2004 by Nancy Gall-Clayton. Reprinted by permission of the author. For additional information please contact the author at 1375 South Second Street, Louisville, Kentucky 40208 or at nancygallclayton@earthlink.net.

The Apostle John by Jeff Goode. Copyright © 2001 by Jeff Goode. Reprinted by permission of the author. For additional information please contact the author at jeffgoode@aol.com.

The Golden Age

Summer by Edward Bond. Copyright © 1992 by Edward Bond. Reprinted by permission of Casarotto Ramsay & Associates Limited. All rights whatsoever in this play are strictly reserved and application for performance etc. must be made before rehearsal to Casarotto Ramsey & Associates Limited, National House, 60-66 Wardour Street, London W1V, 4ND England. No performance may be given unless a license has been obtained.

New Age Voices

About the Editor

Gerald Lee Ratliff is the award-winning author of numerous articles, essays, and textbooks in performance studies and classroom teaching strategies. He has served as President of the Speech and Theatre Association of New Jersey (1983), Eastern Communication Association (1991), Theta Alpha Phi (1986), and the Association for Communication Administration (2002). He has also served on advisory and editorial boards of the American Council of Academic Deans, International Arts Association, National Communication Association, Society of Educators and Scholars, and Eastern Communication Association.

He was awarded the "Distinguished Service Award" by both the Eastern Communication Association (1993) and Theta Alpha Phi (1992); named a Fulbright Scholar to China (1990); selected as U.S.A. delegate of the John F. Kennedy Center for the Performing Arts to Russia (1991); received multiple outstanding teacher awards for pioneering creative approaches in curriculum design and classroom instruction activities; and chaired a number of national commissions in higher education. Most recently, he was named Educator of the Year (2003) by the International Biographical Centre in Cambridge, England, and awarded the prestigious da Vinci Diamond for his contribution to national and international associations.

In addition, he has served as a program consultant and planner for a number of colleges and universities engaged in institutional transformation. He also continues an active schedule of invited workshops and seminars in Reader's Theatre at high schools, colleges, universities, and national conferences. For additional information, please contact him at ratlifgl@potsdam.edu or at (315) 267-2107.

www.ingramcontent.com/pod-product-compliance
Lightning Source LLC
Chambersburg PA
CBHW071853090426
42811CB00004B/586